THIS BOOK BELONGS TO:

_____

STARTING DATE: _____

END DATE: _____

IMPORTANT DATES:

_____

_____

_____

EVERY DAY IS EPIC

A GUIDED JOURNAL FOR
DAYDREAMS, CREATIVE RANTS & BRIGHT IDEAS

MARY KATE McDEVITT

WORKMAN PUBLISHING • NEW YORK

FOR my SISTER, JANE, who CAN TURN ANYTHING INTO an EPIC STORY.

Library of Congress Cataloging-in-Publication Data is available.

ISBN: 978-0-7611-8940-4

Workman books are available at special discounts when purchased in bulk for premiums and sales promotions as well as for fund-raising or educational use. Special editions or book excerpts can also be created to specification. For details, contact the Special Sales Director at the address below, or send an email to specialmarkets@workman.com.

Workman Publishing Co., Inc.

225 Varick Street

New York, NY 10014-4381

workman.com

WORKMAN is a registered trademark of Workman Publishing Co., Inc.

Printed in China

First printing September 2017

10 9 8 7 6 5 4 3 2 1

INTRODUCTION

You may sometimes feel that if you aren't skydiving, cliff-jumping, or living the life of an action-movie stuntperson, your day somehow isn't measuring up. But every day has the potential to be epic (even the days spent doing laundry, or grocery shopping, or binge-watching a new show)—it just comes down to how you frame it. This journal celebrates embracing everyday events—from the mundane to the magnificent—that all add up to something incredibly awesome. Retrace your steps to help tell the day's story. What's something you heard? Who did you see? What did you daydream about? Did you discover a new favorite karaoke jam? The smallest detail can be the thing that totally makes your day, and these pages invite you to find it. And if all you can muster is adding a smile or a frown to record your current mood on a given day, go with it.

The pages are undated (you can fill in dates in the upper corners!), so you can start on any page and at any time—New Year's Day, your birthday, the first day after a big move or milestone, or . . . TODAY!

Date: 4/26

EPIC METER

GENERAL NOTES

- TRIED the NEW CAFE
- MOVED to NEW STUDIO
- MET a BABY named FRITZ
- TRASH-PICKED a PLANT
- BOOKED SUMMER VACAY
- BOUGHT 2 NEW BOOKS
- RESEARCHED DESSERT RECIPES for PICNICS

IN HINDSIGHT...

- SHOULD'VE ORGANIZED the MOVE BETTER
- FOUND A DOG SITTER FIRST
- WOKEN UP EARLIER
- PACKED MORE SNACKS

ALL in ALL, A PRETTY EPIC DAY!

RETRACE your STEPS

EPIC METER

GENERAL NOTES

_____
_____
_____
_____
_____
_____
_____
_____
_____
_____

IN HINDSIGHT...

_____
_____
_____
_____
_____
_____
_____
_____
_____

ALL in ALL, A PRETTY EPIC DAY!

your message here ↘

EPIC METER

GENERAL NOTES

_____
_____
_____
_____
_____
_____
_____
_____
_____
_____

IN HINDSIGHT...

_____
_____
_____
_____
_____
_____
_____
_____

IRON OUT the DETAILS

WORK OUT the KINKS

ALL in ALL, A PRETTY EPIC DAY!

Date: _____

EPIC METER

GENERAL NOTES

_____
_____
_____
_____
_____
_____
_____

IN HINDSIGHT...

_____
_____
_____
_____
_____
_____

ALL *in* ALL,
A PRETTY
EPIC DAY!

MAJOR GROWTH

_____
_____
_____
_____

SEEDLINGS

_____
_____
_____
_____
_____

SHED LIGHT ON *the* SITUATION

UP FOR A
CELEBRATO[RY]
HAND GESTU[RE]
(CIRCLE ON[E])

High 5

Low 5

Too Slo[w]

EPIC RANT

What is going on with...

_____
_____
_____
_____
_____
_____
_____
_____
_____
_____
_____
_____
_____
_____
_____
_____
_____
_____
_____
_____
_____
_____
_____
_____
_____
_____
_____
_____
_____
_____
_____
_____
_____
_____

EPIC METER

GENERAL NOTES

_____
_____
_____
_____
_____
_____
_____
_____
_____

IN HINDSIGHT...

_____
_____
_____
_____
_____
_____
_____

ALL in ALL, A PRETTY EPIC DAY!

Date:_____

EPIC

METER

_____
_____
_____
_____
_____
_____
_____

TODAY'S TAKEAWAY

Date:_____

EPIC

METER

_____
_____
_____
_____
_____
_____
_____

Today's Lesson

Date:_____

EPIC METER

GENERAL NOTES

_____
_____
_____
_____
_____
_____
_____
_____

IN HINDSIGHT...

_____
_____
_____
_____
_____
_____

ALL in ALL, A PRETTY EPIC DAY!

PROS	CONS

WHAT'S THE VERDICT?

SATISFIED WITH THE OUTCOME? YES or NO

RECORD A VICTORY,

ou accomplished enough today!

TODAY WERE YOU SWITCHED ON or OFF?

HOW DIFFICULT WAS IT TO GET FROM POINT Ⓐ to POINT Ⓑ TODAY?

Ⓐ

Ⓑ

TAKE a CLOSER LOOK

EPIC METER

GENERAL NOTES

_____
_____
_____
_____
_____
_____
_____
_____
_____

IN HINDSIGHT...

_____
_____
_____
_____
_____
_____
_____
_____
_____

ALL in ALL, A PRETTY EPIC DAY!

Date:_____

EPIC

METER

GENERAL NOTES

_____
_____
_____
_____
_____
_____
_____
_____
_____

IN HINDSIGHT...

_____
_____
_____
_____
_____
_____
_____
_____
_____

ALL in ALL, A PRETTY EPIC DAY!

HOW FAR DID YOU GET CONQUERING THE DAY?

YAY!

NEARLY THERE...

STARTING is HALF the BATTLE

TODAY'S CHECKLIST

○ GOT STUFF DONE

○ LAUGHED

○ WAS HELPFUL

○ ATE SOMETHING

○ HAD FUN

The
KEY
to
TODAY'S
SUCCESS

BRIGHT IDEAS

EPIC
METER

GENERAL NOTES

_____
_____
_____
_____
_____
_____
_____
_____
_____

IN HINDSIGHT...

_____
_____
_____
_____
_____
_____
_____
_____

ALL in ALL,
A PRETTY
EPIC DAY!

Date:_____

EPIC
METER

_____
_____
_____
_____
_____
_____
_____
_____

SNAP DECISION
maker

#1 _____ #2 _____ #3 _____

NOPE   YASS!   NAH

Date:_____

EPIC
METER

_____
_____
_____
_____
_____
_____
_____
_____
_____

← ↗ ↓

WHERE DID YOU GO?

WHO DID YOU SEE? ↑

↓

↓

WHAT DO YOU KNOW?

→ ↑

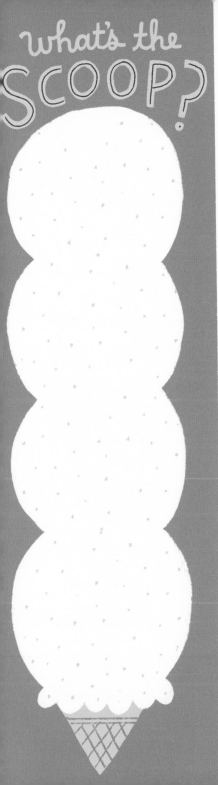

WHAT'S THE SCOOP?

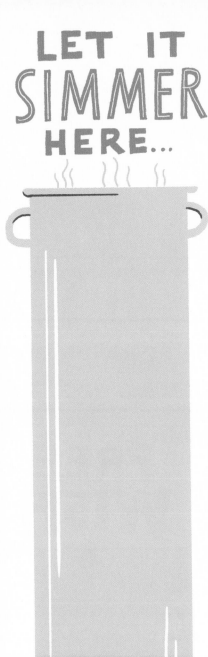

LET IT SIMMER HERE...

EPIC METER

GENERAL NOTES

_____
_____
_____
_____
_____
_____
_____
_____

IN HINDSIGHT...

_____
_____
_____
_____
_____
_____
_____
_____

ALL in ALL, A PRETTY EPIC DAY!

Date: _____

EPIC METER

GENERAL NOTES

_____
_____
_____
_____
_____
_____
_____
_____
_____
_____
_____
_____

IN HINDSIGHT...

_____
_____
_____
_____
_____
_____
_____
_____
_____

ALL in ALL, A PRETTY EPIC DAY!

WHAT WOULD YOU STITCH ON YOUR JEAN JACKET?

FREE WISH

Date: _____

EPIC METER

GENERAL NOTES
_____
_____
_____
_____
_____
_____
_____
_____
_____
_____

IMPORTANT ANNOUNCEMENT!

REQUEST FORM
OFFICIAL DO-OVER REQUEST

IN HINDSIGHT...
_____
_____
_____
_____
_____
_____
_____

REASON:
_____
_____
_____
_____

ALL in ALL, A PRETTY EPIC DAY!

Date:_____

EPIC

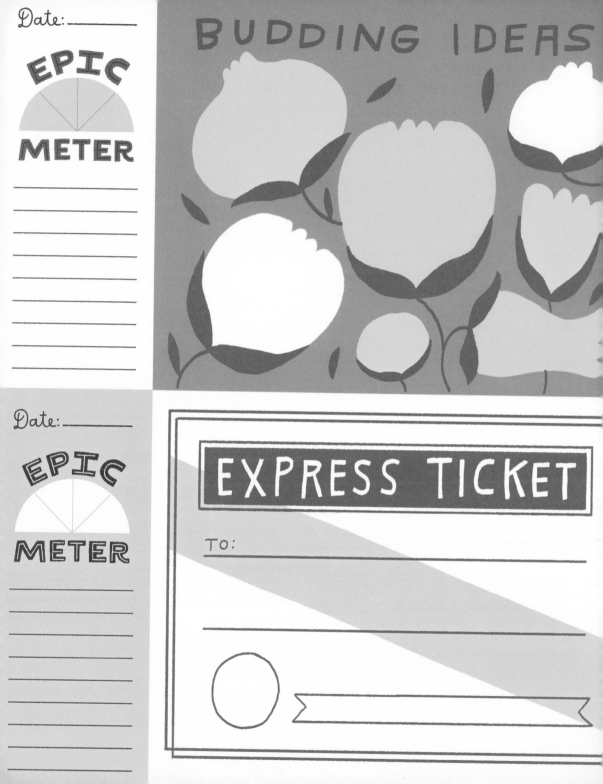

METER

_____
_____
_____
_____
_____
_____
_____
_____
_____

BUDDING IDEAS

Date:_____

EPIC

METER

_____
_____
_____
_____
_____
_____
_____
_____
_____
_____

EXPRESS TICKET

TO: _____

_____

A GOOD TIME to Reflect

Date: _____

EPIC METER

GENERAL NOTES

_____
_____
_____
_____
_____
_____
_____
_____
_____
_____

IN HINDSIGHT...

_____
_____
_____
_____
_____
_____
_____
_____

ALL in ALL, A PRETTY EPIC DAY!

Date:_____

EPIC METER

GENERAL NOTES
_____
_____
_____
_____
_____
_____
_____
_____

IN HINDSIGHT...
_____
_____
_____
_____
_____
_____
_____
_____

ALL in ALL,
A PRETTY
EPIC DAY!

CURRENT MOOD

JUST
YELL it OUT!

HOW DID TODAY MEASURE UP

TODAY _____ YESTERD

PRO TIP:

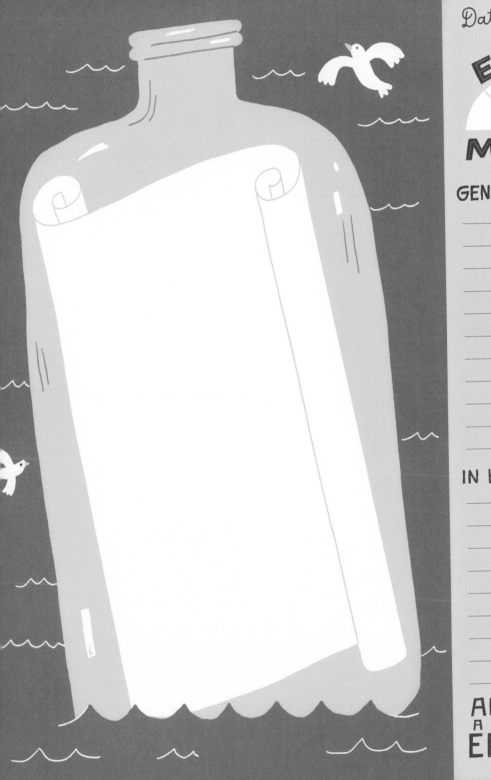

EPIC

METER

GENERAL NOTES

_____
_____
_____
_____
_____
_____
_____
_____
_____
_____
_____

IN HINDSIGHT...

_____
_____
_____
_____
_____
_____
_____
_____

ALL in ALL, A PRETTY EPIC DAY!

Date:_____

EPIC METER

EPIC
METER

GENERAL NOTES

_____
_____
_____
_____
_____
_____
_____
_____

IN HINDSIGHT...

_____
_____
_____
_____
_____
_____
_____
_____

ALL in ALL, A PRETTY EPIC DAY!

HOW IS IT POSSIBLE...

_____
_____
_____
_____
_____
_____
_____
_____
_____
_____
_____
_____
_____
_____
_____
_____
_____

Rant Over.

ON SECOND THOUGHT...

_____
_____
_____
_____
_____
_____
_____

CURRENT DAYDREAMS

IT HAS BEEN

[blank box]

DAYS SINCE THE LAST HAPPY ACCIDENT.

IT'S in the BAG!

CURRENT OBSESSION

Date: _____

EPIC METER

GENERAL NOTES

_____
_____
_____
_____
_____
_____
_____
_____
_____

IN HINDSIGHT...

_____
_____
_____
_____
_____
_____
_____
_____

ALL in ALL, A PRETTY EPIC DAY!

Date:_____

EPIC
METER

GENERAL NOTES

_____
_____
_____
_____
_____
_____
_____
_____
_____

IN HINDSIGHT...

_____
_____
_____
_____
_____
_____
_____

ALL in ALL, A PRETTY EPIC DAY!

CAUTION

AHEAD

OVERHEAR anything INTERESTING TODAY?

INTERESTING
★ OBSERVATION ★
★★   ★★

GROUNDBREAKING
DISCOVERY

FILL 'ER UP!

ONE STEP at a TIME

EPIC METER

EPIC METER

Date: _____

EPIC
METER

GENERAL NOTES

_____
_____
_____
_____
_____
_____
_____

IN HINDSIGHT...

_____
_____
_____
_____
_____

ALL in ALL, A PRETTY EPIC DAY!

Once Upon Today

_____
_____
_____
_____
_____
_____
_____
_____
_____
_____
_____
_____
_____
_____
_____
_____
_____
_____
_____
_____
_____
_____
_____
_____
_____

The End

TODAY'S HEADLINE

EPIC DAILY

3 WISHES

FRIENDS you're ROOTING for

EPIC METER

GENERAL NOTES

IN HINDSIGHT...

ALL in ALL, A PRETTY EPIC DAY!

Date: _____

EPIC
METER

GENERAL NOTES

_____
_____
_____
_____
_____
_____
_____
_____
_____
_____
_____

IN HINDSIGHT...

_____
_____
_____
_____
_____
_____
_____
_____
_____

ALL *in* ALL,
A PRETTY
EPIC DAY!

WRITE IT DOWN

BEFORE YOU FORGET

LEFTOVER PROBLEMS

FILL ANY BIG SHOES TODAY?

OR SMELLY SOCKS?

OR COWBOY BOOTS?

OR BARE FEET?

EPIC METER

GENERAL NOTES

_____
_____
_____
_____
_____
_____
_____
_____
_____
_____

IN HINDSIGHT...

_____
_____
_____
_____
_____
_____
_____
_____
_____

ALL in ALL, A PRETTY EPIC DAY!

EPIC

METER

WHAT YOU SAID:

WHAT YOU ACTUALLY
wanted TO SAY:

WHAT YOU MEANT TO SAY:

EPIC

METER

HIGH NOTES

HARMONY

LOW NOTES

LADDER to SUCCESS

EPIC

METER

GENERAL NOTES

_____
_____
_____
_____
_____
_____
_____
_____
_____
_____

IN HINDSIGHT...

_____
_____
_____
_____
_____
_____
_____

ALL in ALL,
A PRETTY
EPIC DAY!

Date: _____

EPIC
METER

GENERAL NOTES

_____
_____
_____
_____
_____
_____
_____
_____
_____

IN HINDSIGHT...

_____
_____
_____
_____
_____
_____
_____
_____

ALL in ALL, A PRETTY EPIC DAY!

SPECIAL REMINDER

🔍 UPON FURTHER INVESTIGATION

SUBJECT:

EXPLANATION

The RESULT

Could this day get any SWEETER?

_____
_____
_____
_____

Sugar 🍮 🍰 🧁 NEEDS ___ more SPOONFULS

Random Act of Kindness

CAUSES WORTH ROOTING FOR

EPIC METER

GENERAL NOTES
_____
_____
_____
_____
_____
_____
_____
_____
_____
_____
_____
_____
_____

IN HINDSIGHT...
_____
_____
_____
_____
_____
_____
_____

ALL in ALL, A PRETTY EPIC DAY!

Date: _____

EPIC

METER

GENERAL NOTES

_____
_____
_____
_____
_____
_____
_____
_____
_____
_____
_____

IN HINDSIGHT...

_____
_____
_____
_____
_____
_____
_____
_____
_____
_____

**ALL in ALL,
A PRETTY
EPIC DAY!**

EPIC RANT

REALLY?! REALLY.

RANT OVER.

SPECIAL KEEPSAKE

NAME THIS CAT

_____

EPIC METER

GENERAL NOTES

_____
_____
_____
_____
_____
_____
_____
_____

ITEMS THAT ARE STILL LOST

MYSTERIOUSLY MISSING ↗

NEVER LENDING MY STUFF AGAIN...

↖ MISS that ONE...

↖ WHERE COULD IT BE?!

WHY?

HMM...

NOW THAT'S A REASON TO CELEBRATE!

IN HINDSIGHT...

_____
_____
_____
_____
_____
_____
_____

ALL in ALL, A PRETTY EPIC DAY!

Date: _____

EPIC

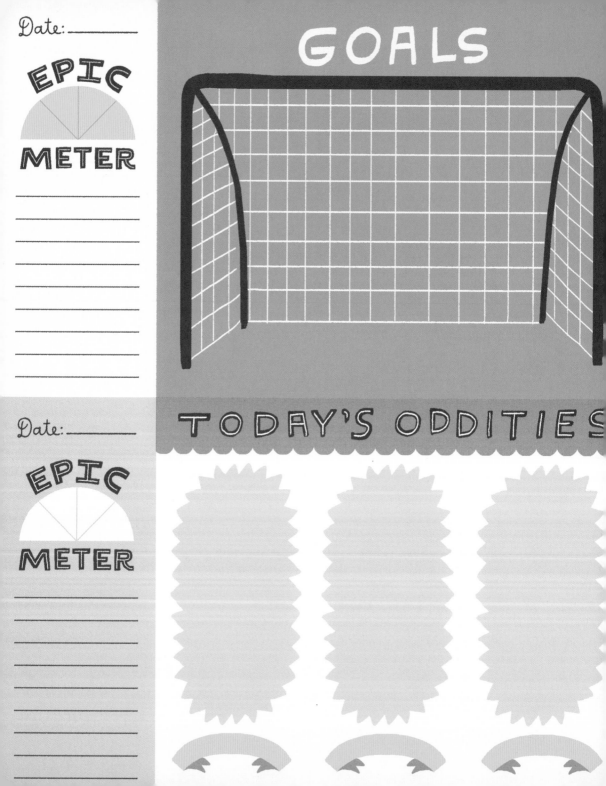

METER

_____
_____
_____
_____
_____
_____
_____
_____
_____

GOALS

Date: _____

EPIC

METER

_____
_____
_____
_____
_____
_____
_____
_____

TODAY'S ODDITIES

Let it SOAK in...

EPIC METER

GENERAL NOTES

_____
_____
_____
_____
_____
_____
_____
_____
_____
_____
_____

IN HINDSIGHT...

_____
_____
_____
_____
_____
_____
_____
_____

ALL in ALL, A PRETTY EPIC DAY!

Date: _____

EPIC METER

GENERAL NOTES

_____
_____
_____
_____
_____
_____
_____
_____

IN HINDSIGHT...

_____
_____
_____
_____
_____
_____
_____

ALL in ALL,
A PRETTY
EPIC DAY!

TODAY'S ACCOMPLISHMENT

PROBLEM-REPAIR-SHOP QUEU

Nothing is unfixable!

TRY to WALK in SOMEONE ELSE'S SHOES

Learn anything on the journey?

_____
_____
_____
_____

HOW did TODAY START?

HOW did TODAY END?

IS EVERYTHING ORGANIZED?

EPIC METER

GENERAL NOTES

_____
_____
_____
_____
_____
_____
_____
_____
_____
_____
_____

IN HINDSIGHT...

_____
_____
_____
_____
_____
_____
_____
_____
_____

ALL in ALL, A PRETTY EPIC DAY!

Date: _____

EPIC
METER

GENERAL NOTES

_____
_____
_____
_____
_____
_____
_____
_____
_____

IN HINDSIGHT...

_____
_____
_____
_____
_____
_____
_____

ALL in ALL,
A PRETTY
EPIC DAY!

LIE AWAKE THINKING

Fond Memory

TODAY'S LOG

COUNT YOUR LUCKY STARS

EPIC

METER

_____
_____
_____
_____
_____
_____
_____
_____

SARDINES

JAM-PACKED DAY

EPIC

METER

_____
_____
_____
_____
_____
_____
_____

Date: _____

EPIC

METER

GENERAL NOTES

_____
_____
_____
_____
_____
_____
_____
_____
_____
_____
_____
_____
_____
_____

IN HINDSIGHT...

_____
_____
_____
_____
_____
_____
_____
_____
_____

ALL in ALL, A PRETTY EPIC DAY!

PERFORMANCE RANKING

_____ ROOKIE

_____ NOVICE

_____ EXPERT

_____ VETERAN

_____ GRIZZLED

HATS OFF TO YOU

Today's Specials

YOUR 2¢

Greetings from... SUNNY · RAINY · BORING · EXPENSIVE

_____

WHERE I LEARNED THAT...

_____

EPIC METER

GENERAL NOTES

_____
_____
_____
_____
_____
_____
_____
_____
_____
_____
_____
_____
_____

IN HINDSIGHT...

_____
_____
_____
_____
_____
_____
_____
_____

ALL in ALL, A PRETTY EPIC DAY!

EPIC RANT

SING IT!

WORD OF THE DAY

Date: _____

EPIC

(semi-circle meter graphic)

METER

GENERAL NOTES

_____
_____
_____
_____
_____
_____
_____
_____
_____

IN HINDSIGHT...

_____
_____
_____
_____
_____
_____
_____
_____

ALL *in* ALL,
A PRETTY
EPIC DAY!

BREAKING NEWS

BULLETIN BOARD

LOST

WANTED

FOUND

TODAY, SUMMED UP IN PANTS

STAINED
SWEATPANTS

SENSIBLE
SLACKS

Sexy *leather* *pants*

MESSAGE to the WORLD!

EPIC

METER

GENERAL NOTES

IN HINDSIGHT...

ALL in ALL,
A PRETTY
EPIC DAY!

Date: _____

EPIC
METER

GENERAL NOTES

_____
_____
_____
_____
_____
_____
_____
_____
_____
_____
_____

IN HINDSIGHT...

_____
_____
_____
_____
_____
_____
_____
_____

ALL in ALL,
A PRETTY
EPIC DAY!

MOOD FORECAST

WORLD'S BEST

_____

CURRENT KARAOKE JAM

TOMORROW'S PREDICTION

WRITE THE FIRST THING THAT POPS INTO YOUR HEAD.

EPIC

METER

_____
_____
_____
_____
_____
_____
_____
_____

YUCK!   YUM!

EPIC

METER

_____
_____
_____
_____
_____
_____
_____
_____
_____

Date:_____

EPIC

METER

GENERAL NOTES

_____
_____
_____
_____
_____
_____
_____
_____
_____
_____
_____
_____
_____

IN HINDSIGHT...

_____
_____
_____
_____
_____
_____
_____
_____
_____
_____

**ALL in ALL,
A PRETTY
EPIC DAY!**

VENT HERE

○ _____ _____
_____ _____
_____ _____
_____ _____
○ _____ _____

ACCOMPLISHMENTS

MAJOR	MINOR	MEH

HOW CLOSE TO THE TARGET WERE YOU TODAY?

EPIC RANT

EVERYONE SHOULD...

Date: _____

EPIC METER

GENERAL NOTES

_____
_____
_____
_____
_____
_____
_____
_____
_____
_____

IN HINDSIGHT...

_____
_____
_____
_____
_____
_____
_____

SPICE up THE DAY!

ALL in ALL, A PRETTY EPIC DAY!

EPIC

METER

GENERAL NOTES

_____
_____
_____
_____

_____
_____
_____

_____
_____
_____

IN HINDSIGHT...

_____
_____
_____

_____
_____
_____

_____
_____

ALL in ALL, A PRETTY EPIC DAY!

EPIC RANT

Why do we STILL...

RANT OVER.

ADVICE COLUMN

FEELING STUMPED

IMMENSE PROBLEMS

Date: _____

EPIC METER

GENERAL NOTES

_____
_____
_____
_____
_____
_____
_____
_____
_____

IN HINDSIGHT...

_____
_____
_____
_____
_____
_____
_____

ALL in ALL, A PRETTY EPIC DAY!

Date:_____

EPIC
METER

_____
_____
_____
_____
_____
_____
_____
_____

TODAY'S TAKEAWAY

Date:_____

EPIC
METER

_____
_____
_____
_____
_____
_____
_____
_____

Today's Lesson

TODAY'S TOP 10

10
9
8
7
6
5
4
3
2
1

PRO TIP:

CURRENT OBSESSION

what are we celebrating?

EPIC METER

GENERAL NOTES

IN HINDSIGHT...

ALL in ALL, A PRETTY EPIC DAY!

Date:_____

EPIC METER

GENERAL NOTES

_____
_____
_____
_____
_____
_____
_____
_____
_____
_____
_____

IN HINDSIGHT...

_____
_____
_____
_____
_____
_____
_____
_____
_____

ALL *in* ALL,
A PRETTY
EPIC DAY!

RETRACE *your* STEPS!

START

1

2

3

4

5

6

7

END

DA BOMB or TODAY BOMBED IT?

CURRENT OBSESSION

EPIC METER

GENERAL NOTES

BIG Announcement

IN HINDSIGHT...

WAS THE GLASS...
- HALF-FULL?
- HALF-EMPTY?
- OVERFLOWING?
- BONE-DRY?

ALL in ALL, A PRETTY EPIC DAY!

Date:_____

EPIC METER

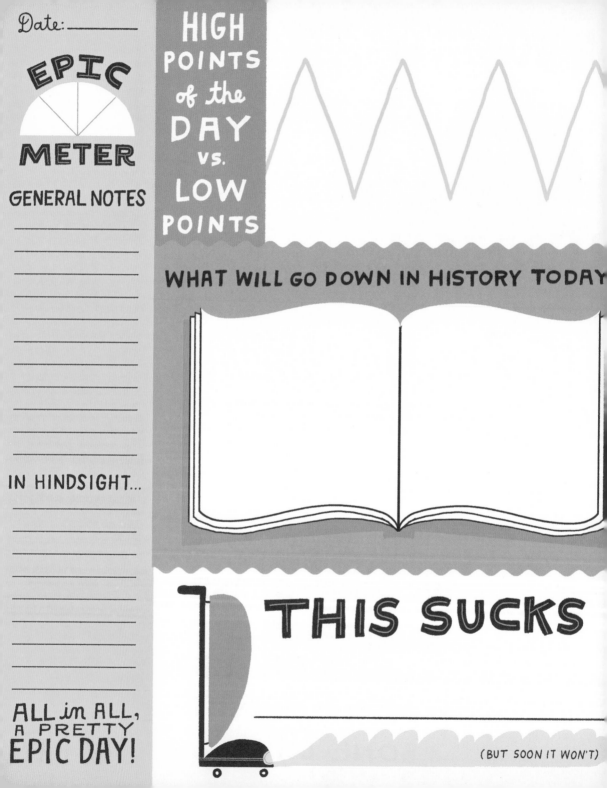

GENERAL NOTES

_____
_____
_____
_____
_____
_____
_____
_____
_____
_____

IN HINDSIGHT...

_____
_____
_____
_____
_____
_____
_____
_____

ALL *in* ALL, A PRETTY EPIC DAY!

HIGH POINTS *of the* DAY *vs.* LOW POINTS

WHAT WILL GO DOWN IN HISTORY TODAY

THIS SUCKS

_____

(BUT SOON IT WON'T)

CERTIFICATE

OF

TODAY'S
ACCOMPLISHMENTS

Date: _____

EPIC

METER

GENERAL NOTES

_____
_____
_____
_____
_____
_____
_____
_____
_____

IN HINDSIGHT...

_____
_____
_____
_____
_____
_____
_____

ALL *in* ALL,
A PRETTY
EPIC DAY!

Date:_____

EPIC
METER

_____
_____
_____
_____
_____
_____
_____
_____

GOALS

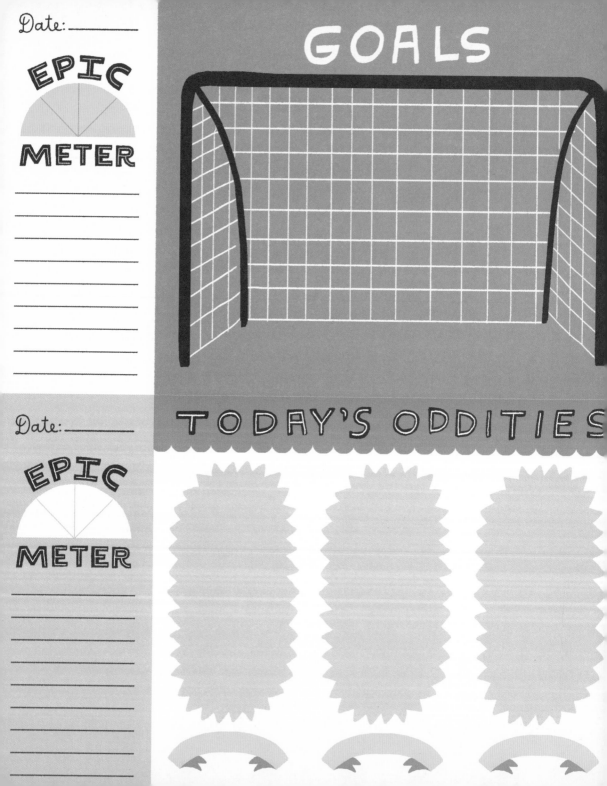

Date:_____

EPIC
METER

_____
_____
_____
_____
_____
_____
_____
_____

TODAY'S ODDITIES

A NEW PERSPECTIVE

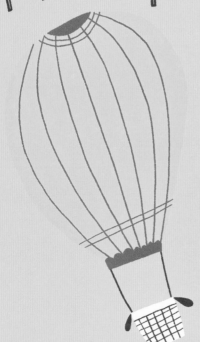

EPIC METER

GENERAL NOTES

_____
_____
_____
_____
_____
_____
_____
_____
_____
_____
_____

IN HINDSIGHT...

_____
_____
_____
_____
_____
_____
_____
_____

ALL *in* ALL, A PRETTY EPIC DAY!

Date: _____

EPIC METER

GENERAL NOTES

_____
_____
_____
_____
_____
_____
_____
_____
_____
_____

IN HINDSIGHT...

_____
_____
_____
_____
_____
_____
_____

ALL *in* ALL,
A PRETTY
EPIC DAY!

SOMETHING YOU'VE BEEN MEANING TO GET OFF YOUR BACK:

when life hands you LEMONS, turn them INTO...

TODAY COULD'VE USED AN ⋅⋅ AUTOMATED ⋅⋅

01

Where WOULD you HEAD on the OPEN ROAD?

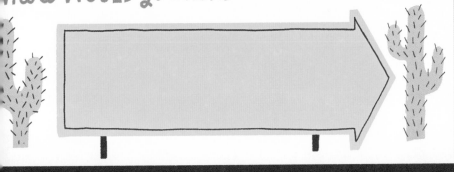

EPIC

METER

GENERAL NOTES

_____
_____
_____
_____
_____
_____
_____
_____

IN HINDSIGHT...

_____
_____
_____
_____
_____
_____
_____
_____
_____

ALL in ALL, A PRETTY EPIC DAY!

Date:_____

EPIC METER

GENERAL NOTES

_____
_____
_____
_____
_____
_____
_____
_____
_____
_____

IN HINDSIGHT...

_____
_____
_____
_____
_____
_____
_____
_____
_____
_____

ALL in ALL, A PRETTY EPIC DAY!

WISH LIST

SH*T LIST

WHEN THE PLANETS ALIGN

_____
_____
_____
_____

COUNT YOUR LUCKY STARS

EPIC
METER

EPIC
METER

SARDINES
JAM-PACKED DAY

Date: _____

EPIC METER

GENERAL NOTES

_____
_____
_____
_____
_____
_____
_____
_____

IN HINDSIGHT...

_____
_____
_____
_____
_____
_____
_____

ALL in ALL, A PRETTY EPIC DAY!

JUST PUTTING THIS OUT THERE...

TODAY'S
TOP 10

10
9
8
7
6
5
4
3
2
1

CURRENT OBSESSION

EPIC
METER

GENERAL NOTES

_____
_____
_____
_____
_____
_____
_____
_____
_____

IN HINDSIGHT...

_____
_____
_____
_____
_____
_____
_____

what are we "celebrating?"

ALL in ALL, A PRETTY EPIC DAY!

EPIC
METER

GENERAL NOTES

_____
_____
_____
_____
_____
_____
_____
_____

IN HINDSIGHT...

_____
_____
_____
_____
_____
_____
_____

ALL in ALL,
A PRETTY
EPIC DAY!

NOTEWORTHY NEWS

_____

_____

HEY! WHAT'S COOKIN'?

WELL-DONE	HALF-BAKED	OVERDON

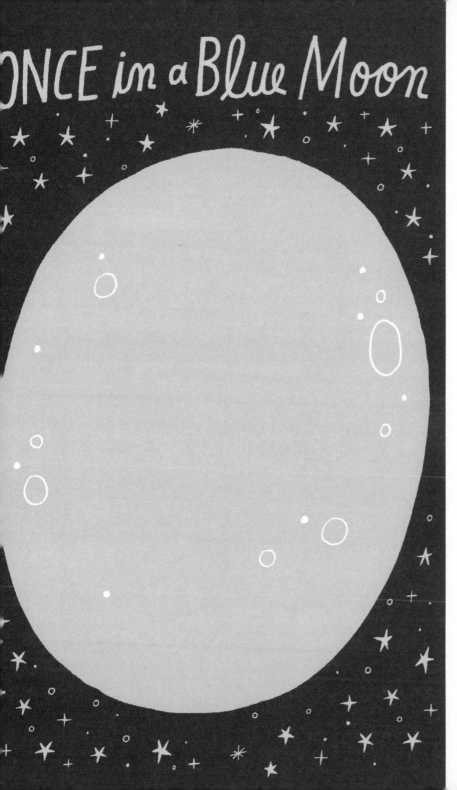

ONCE in a Blue Moon

EPIC
METER

GENERAL NOTES

_____
_____
_____
_____
_____
_____
_____
_____
_____

IN HINDSIGHT...

_____
_____
_____
_____
_____
_____
_____
_____

ALL in ALL,
A PRETTY
EPIC DAY!

Date:_____

EPIC METER

_____
_____
_____
_____
_____
_____
_____
_____

IN HINDSIGHT...

_____
_____
_____
_____
_____
_____
_____

ALL *in* ALL,
A PRETTY
EPIC DAY!

FUTURE BUSINESSES

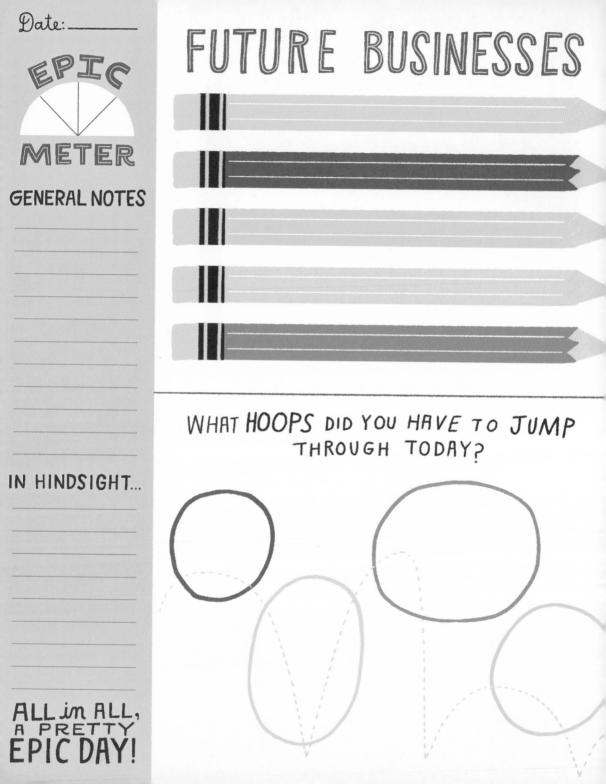

WHAT **HOOPS** DID YOU HAVE TO JUMP THROUGH TODAY?

BUDDING IDEAS

EPIC

METER

EPIC

METER

EXPRESS TICKET

TO: _____

_____

Date: _____

EPIC METER

GENERAL NOTES
_____
_____
_____
_____
_____
_____
_____
_____
_____
_____
_____

IN HINDSIGHT...
_____
_____
_____
_____
_____
_____
_____
_____

ALL in ALL, A PRETTY EPIC DAY!

FRUITS of YOUR LABOR

WALL of FAME

WALL of SHAME

DEEP THOUGHTS

SHIPWRECKS

BURIED TREASURE

EPIC

METER

GENERAL NOTES

IN HINDSIGHT...

ALL in ALL, A PRETTY EPIC DAY!

Date:_____

EPIC METER

GENERAL NOTES

_____
_____
_____
_____
_____
_____
_____
_____

IN HINDSIGHT...

_____
_____
_____
_____
_____
_____
_____
_____
_____

ALL in ALL, A PRETTY EPIC DAY!

STEPPING STONES

BUILDING BLOCKS

LOOKING FORWARD TO...

OFFICIAL COUNTDOWN

(YOUR MESSAGE HERE)

ORGANIZE YOUR
THOUGHTS

EPIC
METER

GENERAL NOTES

_____
_____
_____
_____
_____
_____
_____
_____
_____

IN HINDSIGHT...

_____
_____
_____
_____
_____
_____
_____
_____

ALL in ALL,
A PRETTY
EPIC DAY!

Date:_____

EPIC

METER

_____
_____
_____
_____
_____
_____
_____
_____

SNAP DECISION
maker

#1 [____] #2 [____] #3 [____]

NOPE   YASS!   NAH

Date:_____

EPIC

METER

_____
_____
_____
_____
_____
_____
_____
_____

WHERE DID YOU GO?

WHO DID YOU SEE?

WHAT DO YOU KNOW?

The TITLE of TODAY'S BOOK   The TITLE of YESTERDAY'S BOOK

EPIC
METER

GENERAL NOTES

WHICH TOOL WILL REPAIR TODAY? (CIRCLE ONE)

IN HINDSIGHT...

THE TUNNEL

THE LIGHT
at the END of IT

ALL in ALL,
A PRETTY
EPIC DAY!

Date: _____

EPIC METER

GENERAL NOTES

_____
_____
_____
_____
_____
_____
_____
_____
_____
_____

IN HINDSIGHT...

_____
_____
_____
_____
_____
_____
_____
_____
_____
_____
_____

ALL *in* ALL,
A PRETTY
EPIC DAY!

Recipe for SUCCESS

With a DASH of →
and a PINCH of →

Recipe for DISASTER

ADD a TOUCH of →
and TOP with

AIR YOUR GRIEVANCES

LIFE REPORT CARD

A-DOING GREAT B-NOT BAD C-NEEDS IMPROVEMENT D-THAT DIDN'T GO WELL F-UGHH!!

SUBJECT	GRADE

Extra Credit

EPIC METER

GENERAL NOTES

_____
_____
_____
_____
_____
_____
_____
_____
_____

IN HINDSIGHT...

_____
_____
_____
_____
_____
_____
_____
_____
_____

ALL *in* ALL,
A PRETTY
EPIC DAY!

Date: _____

EPIC METER

GENERAL NOTES

_____
_____
_____
_____
_____
_____
_____
_____

IN HINDSIGHT...

_____
_____
_____
_____
_____
_____
_____
_____
_____

ALL *in* ALL,
A PRETTY
EPIC DAY!

WINDOWS OF OPPORTUNITY

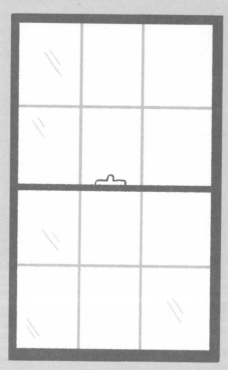

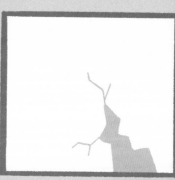

IT WAS THE BEST OF TIMES

IT WAS THE WORST OF TIMES

TODAY'S GOOD EGGS

TODAY'S BAD APPLES

Date: _____

EPIC METER

GENERAL NOTES

_____
_____
_____
_____
_____
_____
_____
_____

IN HINDSIGHT...

_____
_____
_____
_____
_____
_____
_____

ALL *in* ALL,
A PRETTY
EPIC DAY!

Let it SOAK in...

EPIC METER

GENERAL NOTES

_____
_____
_____
_____
_____
_____
_____
_____
_____

IN HINDSIGHT...

_____
_____
_____
_____
_____
_____
_____
_____
_____

ALL in ALL,
A PRETTY
EPIC DAY!

Date: _____

EPIC
METER

GENERAL NOTES

_____
_____
_____
_____
_____
_____
_____
_____

IN HINDSIGHT...

_____
_____
_____
_____
_____
_____
_____
_____
_____
_____

ALL *in* ALL,
A PRETTY
EPIC DAY!

your message here ↘

EPIC METER

GENERAL NOTES
_____
_____
_____
_____
_____
_____
_____

IN HINDSIGHT...
_____
_____
_____
_____
_____

ALL in ALL, A PRETTY EPIC DAY!

IRON OUT the DETAILS

WORK OUT the KINKS

Date:_____

EPIC METER

GENERAL NOTES
_____
_____
_____
_____
_____
_____
_____
_____
_____

IN HINDSIGHT...
_____
_____
_____
_____
_____
_____
_____
_____
_____

ALL in ALL, A PRETTY EPIC DAY!

MAJOR GROWTH
_____
_____
_____
_____
_____

SEEDLINGS
_____
_____
_____
_____
_____

SHED LIGHT ON the SITUATION

UP FOR A CELEBRATOR
HAND GESTUR
(CIRCLE ON

High 5

Low 5

Too Slow

EPIC RANT

What is going on with...

_____
_____
_____
_____
_____
_____
_____
_____
_____
_____
_____
_____
_____
_____
_____
_____
_____
_____
_____
_____
_____
_____
_____
_____
_____
_____
_____
_____
_____
_____
_____
_____

EPIC METER

GENERAL NOTES

_____
_____
_____
_____
_____
_____
_____
_____
_____

IN HINDSIGHT...

_____
_____
_____
_____
_____
_____
_____
_____

ALL in ALL, A PRETTY EPIC DAY!

Date:_____

EPIC
METER

_____
_____
_____
_____
_____
_____
_____
_____

TODAY'S TAKEAWAY

Date:_____

EPIC
METER

_____
_____
_____
_____
_____
_____
_____
_____

Today's Lesson

HOW ABOUT THESE APPLES?

Date: _____

EPIC METER

GENERAL NOTES

IN HINDSIGHT...

ALL in ALL, A PRETTY EPIC DAY!

Date: _____

EPIC

METER

GENERAL NOTES

_____
_____
_____
_____
_____
_____
_____
_____

IN HINDSIGHT...

_____
_____
_____
_____
_____
_____
_____

ALL in ALL, A PRETTY EPIC DAY!

The ULTIMATE DECISION

PROS	CONS

WHAT'S THE VERDICT

SATISFIED WITH THE OUTCOME? YES or N

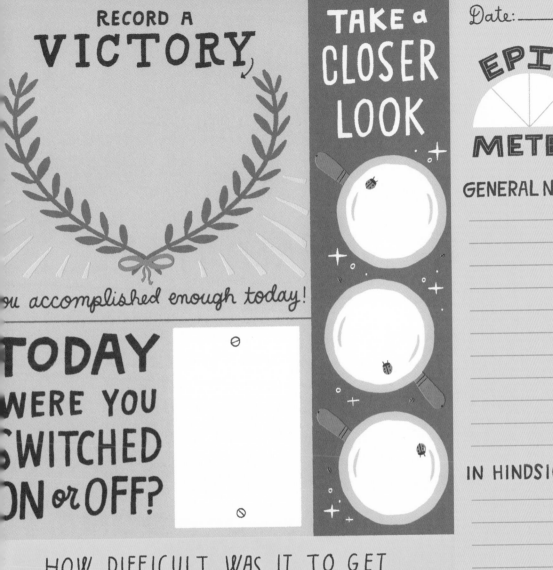

RECORD A VICTORY,

...ou accomplished enough today!

TODAY WERE YOU SWITCHED ON or OFF?

HOW DIFFICULT WAS IT TO GET FROM POINT Ⓐ to POINT Ⓑ TODAY?

Ⓐ

Ⓑ

TAKE a CLOSER LOOK

Date:_____

EPIC METER

GENERAL NOTES

_____
_____
_____
_____
_____
_____
_____

IN HINDSIGHT...

_____
_____
_____
_____
_____
_____
_____
_____

ALL in ALL,
A PRETTY
EPIC DAY!

Date:_____

EPIC METER

GENERAL NOTES

_____
_____
_____
_____
_____
_____

IN HINDSIGHT...

_____
_____
_____
_____
_____
_____
_____

ALL in ALL,
A PRETTY
EPIC DAY!

HOW FAR DID YOU GET CONQUERING THE DAY?

YAY!

NEARLY THERE...

STARTING is HALF the BATTLE

TODAY'S CHECKLIST

- ○ GOT STUFF DONE
- ○ LAUGHED
- ○ WAS HELPFUL
- ○ ATE SOMETHING
- ○ HAD FUN

The
KEY
to
TODAY'S

SUCCESS

BRIGHT IDEAS

GENERAL NOTES
_____
_____
_____
_____
_____
_____
_____
_____
_____

IN HINDSIGHT...
_____
_____
_____
_____
_____
_____
_____

ALL in ALL,
A PRETTY
EPIC DAY!

Date:_____

EPIC
METER

_____
_____
_____
_____
_____
_____
_____

SNAP DECISION
maker

#1 _____ #2 _____ #3 _____

NOPE   YASS!   NAH

Date:_____

EPIC
METER

_____
_____
_____
_____
_____
_____
_____

WHERE DID YOU GO?

WHO DID YOU SEE?

WHAT DO YOU KNOW?

what's the SCOOP?

LET IT SIMMER HERE...

Date: _____

EPIC METER

GENERAL NOTES

_____
_____
_____
_____
_____
_____
_____
_____
_____
_____
_____

IN HINDSIGHT...

_____
_____
_____
_____
_____
_____
_____
_____

ALL in ALL, A PRETTY EPIC DAY!

EPIC METER

GENERAL NOTES

_____
_____
_____
_____
_____
_____
_____
_____
_____

IN HINDSIGHT...

_____
_____
_____
_____
_____
_____
_____

ALL in ALL, A PRETTY EPIC DAY!

WHAT WOULD YOU STITCH ON YOUR JEAN JACKET?

FREE WISH

Date: _____

IMPORTANT ANNOUNCEMENT!

EPIC METER

GENERAL NOTES

_____
_____
_____
_____
_____
_____
_____
_____
_____
_____

REQUEST FORM
= OFFICIAL DO-OVER REQUEST =

IN HINDSIGHT...

_____
_____
_____
_____

REASON:

_____
_____
_____
_____

ALL in ALL, A PRETTY EPIC DAY!

Date:_____

EPIC

METER

_____
_____
_____
_____
_____
_____
_____
_____

Date:_____

EPIC
METER

_____
_____
_____
_____
_____
_____
_____
_____

EXPRESS TICKET

TO:_____

_____

A GOOD TIME to Reflect

EPIC METER

GENERAL NOTES

_____
_____
_____
_____
_____
_____
_____
_____
_____
_____
_____
_____

IN HINDSIGHT...

_____
_____
_____
_____
_____
_____
_____

ALL in ALL, A PRETTY EPIC DAY!

Date: _____

EPIC

METER

GENERAL NOTES

_____
_____
_____
_____
_____
_____
_____
_____
_____
_____
_____

IN HINDSIGHT...

_____
_____
_____
_____
_____
_____
_____
_____

ALL *in* ALL,
A PRETTY
EPIC DAY!

CURRENT MOOD

JUST YELL *it* OUT!

PRO TIP:

TODAY _____   YESTERD

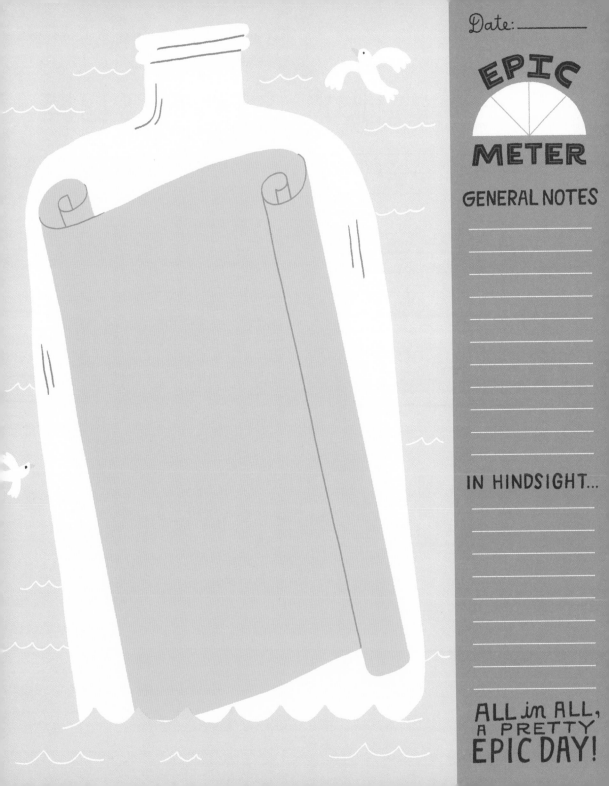

EPIC
METER

GENERAL NOTES

_____
_____
_____
_____
_____
_____
_____
_____
_____
_____
_____

IN HINDSIGHT...

_____
_____
_____
_____
_____
_____
_____
_____
_____

ALL in ALL,
A PRETTY
EPIC DAY!

Date:_____

EPIC METER

GENERAL NOTES

_____
_____
_____
_____
_____
_____
_____
_____
_____
_____

IN HINDSIGHT...

_____
_____
_____
_____
_____
_____
_____
_____

ALL in ALL, A PRETTY EPIC DAY!

EPIC RANT

HOW IS IT POSSIBLE...

_____
_____
_____
_____
_____
_____
_____
_____
_____
_____
_____
_____
_____
_____
_____
_____

Rant Over.

ON SECOND THOUGHT...

_____
_____
_____
_____
_____
_____
_____

CURRENT DAYDREAMS

IT HAS BEEN

DAYS SINCE THE LAST HAPPY ACCIDENT.

IT'S in the BAG!

CURRENT OBSESSION

EPIC METER

GENERAL NOTES

IN HINDSIGHT...

ALL in ALL, A PRETTY EPIC DAY!

Date:_____

EPIC
METER

GENERAL NOTES

_____
_____
_____
_____
_____
_____
_____
_____

IN HINDSIGHT...

_____
_____
_____
_____
_____
_____
_____

ALL in ALL,
A PRETTY
EPIC DAY!

CAUTION

AHEAD

OVERHEAR anything INTERESTING TODAY?

INTERESTING
★ OBSERVATION ★

GROUNDBREAKING
DISCOVERY

FILL 'ER UP!

EPIC
METER

ONE
STEP at a
TIME

EPIC
METER

Date: _____

EPIC METER

GENERAL NOTES
_____
_____
_____
_____
_____
_____
_____
_____
_____

IN HINDSIGHT...
_____
_____
_____
_____
_____
_____
_____

ALL in ALL,
A PRETTY
EPIC DAY!

Once Upon Today

_____
_____
_____
_____
_____
_____
_____
_____
_____
_____
_____
_____
_____
_____
_____
_____
_____
_____
_____
_____
_____

The End

TODAY'S HEADLINE

EPIC DAILY

3 WISHES

FRIENDS you're ROOTING for

EPIC METER

GENERAL NOTES

IN HINDSIGHT...

ALL in ALL, A PRETTY EPIC DAY!

Date: _____

EPIC
METER

GENERAL NOTES

_____
_____
_____
_____
_____
_____
_____
_____
_____
_____
_____

IN HINDSIGHT...

_____
_____
_____
_____
_____
_____
_____
_____
_____
_____

ALL in ALL, A PRETTY EPIC DAY!

BIG PLANS

WRITE IT DOWN

BEFORE YOU FORGET

LEFTOVER PROBLEMS

EPIC

METER

GENERAL NOTES

_____
_____
_____
_____
_____
_____
_____
_____
_____
_____

IN HINDSIGHT...

_____
_____
_____
_____
_____
_____
_____
_____
_____

FILL ANY BIG SHOES TODAY?

OR SMELLY SOCKS?

OR BARE FEET?

OR COWBOY BOOTS?

ALL *in* ALL, A PRETTY EPIC DAY!

Date:_____

EPIC
METER

_____
_____
_____
_____
_____
_____
_____
_____

WHAT YOU SAID:

WHAT YOU ACTUALLY
wanted TO SAY:

WHAT YOU MEANT TO SAY:

Date:_____

EPIC
METER

_____
_____
_____
_____
_____
_____
_____
_____

HIGH NOTES

HARMONY

LOW NOTES

LADDER to SUCCESS

EPIC METER

GENERAL NOTES

_____
_____
_____
_____
_____
_____
_____
_____
_____
_____
_____

IN HINDSIGHT...

_____
_____
_____
_____
_____
_____
_____
_____
_____

ALL in ALL, A PRETTY EPIC DAY!

Date:_____

EPIC

METER

GENERAL NOTES

_____
_____
_____
_____
_____
_____
_____
_____
_____
_____
_____

IN HINDSIGHT...

_____
_____
_____
_____
_____
_____
_____
_____

ALL in ALL, A PRETTY EPIC DAY!

SPECIAL REMINDER

🔍 UPON FURTHER INVESTIGATION

SUBJECT:

EXPLANATION

The RESULT

Could this day get any SWEETER?

_____
_____
_____

Sugar

NEEDS ___ more SPOONFULS

Random Act of Kindness

CAUSES WORTH ROOTING FOR

EPIC METER

GENERAL NOTES

_____
_____
_____
_____
_____
_____
_____
_____
_____
_____

IN HINDSIGHT...

_____
_____
_____
_____
_____
_____
_____
_____

ALL in ALL, A PRETTY EPIC DAY!

Date: _____

EPIC METER

GENERAL NOTES

_____
_____
_____
_____
_____
_____
_____
_____
_____
_____

IN HINDSIGHT...

_____
_____
_____
_____
_____
_____
_____
_____

ALL in ALL, A PRETTY EPIC DAY!

REALLY?! REALLY.

RANT OVER.

SPECIAL KEEPSAKE

NAME THIS CAT

_____

EPIC METER

GENERAL NOTES

_____
_____
_____
_____
_____
_____
_____
_____

ITEMS THAT ARE STILL LOST

MYSTERIOUSLY MISSING ↗
_____

↖ MISS that ONE...
_____

WHY?

NEVER LENDING MY STUFF AGAIN...
_____

↖ WHERE COULD IT BE?!
_____

HMM...

IN HINDSIGHT...

_____
_____
_____
_____
_____
_____
_____
_____
_____
_____
_____

NOW THAT'S A REASON TO CELEBRATE!

ALL in ALL, A PRETTY EPIC DAY!

Date:_____

EPIC

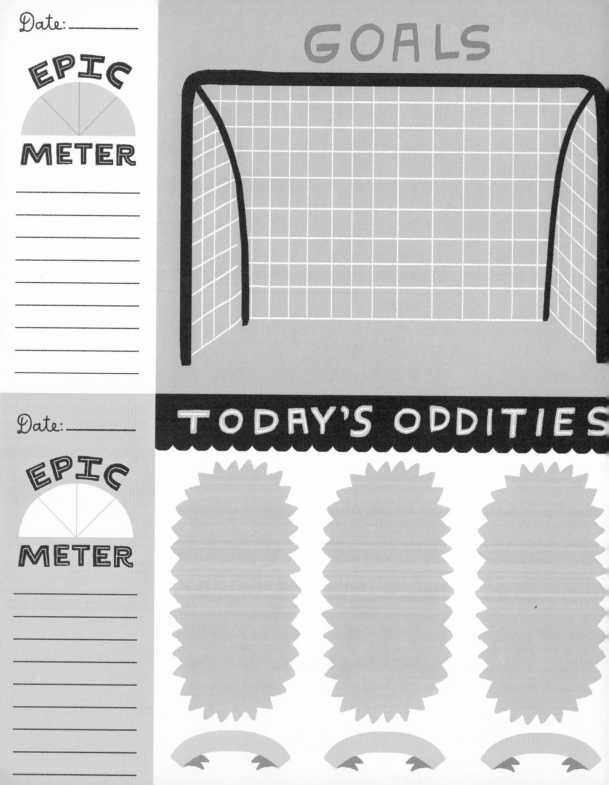

METER

_____
_____
_____
_____
_____
_____
_____
_____
_____

GOALS

Date:_____

EPIC

METER

_____
_____
_____
_____
_____
_____
_____
_____
_____

TODAY'S ODDITIES

Let it SOAK in...

EPIC
METER

GENERAL NOTES

_____
_____
_____
_____
_____
_____
_____
_____
_____
_____
_____
_____

IN HINDSIGHT...

_____
_____
_____
_____
_____
_____
_____
_____

ALL in ALL,
A PRETTY
EPIC DAY!

Date: _____

EPIC METER

GENERAL NOTES

_____
_____
_____
_____
_____
_____
_____
_____
_____

IN HINDSIGHT...

_____
_____
_____
_____
_____
_____
_____
_____

ALL *in* ALL,
A PRETTY
EPIC DAY!

TODAY'S ACCOMPLISHMENT

PROBLEM-REPAIR-SHOP QUEU

_____
_____
_____
_____
_____

Nothing is unfixable!

TRY to WALK in SOMEONE ELSE'S SHOES

Learn anything on the journey?

HOW did TODAY **START?**

HOW did TODAY **END?**

IS EVERYTHING ORGANIZED?

EPIC METER

GENERAL NOTES

IN HINDSIGHT...

ALL in ALL, A PRETTY EPIC DAY!

Date: _____

EPIC METER

GENERAL NOTES

_____
_____
_____
_____
_____
_____
_____
_____
_____
_____

IN HINDSIGHT...

_____
_____
_____
_____
_____
_____
_____

ALL in ALL, A PRETTY EPIC DAY!

LIE AWAKE THINKING

Fond Memory

TODAY'S LOG

COUNT YOUR LUCKY STARS

EPIC
METER

_____
_____
_____
_____
_____
_____

SARDINES
JAM-PACKED DAY

EPIC
METER

_____
_____
_____
_____
_____
_____

Date: _____

EPIC METER

GENERAL NOTES

_____
_____
_____
_____
_____
_____
_____
_____

IN HINDSIGHT...

_____
_____
_____
_____
_____
_____

ALL in ALL, A PRETTY EPIC DAY!

PERFORMANCE ★RANKING★

_____ ROOKIE

_____ NOVICE

_____ EXPERT

_____ VETERAN

_____ GRIZZLED

HATS OFF TO YOU

Today's Specials

YOUR 2¢

Greetings · SUNNY · RAINY
from... · BORING · EXPENSIVE

_____

WHERE I LEARNED THAT...

_____

EPIC
METER

GENERAL NOTES
_____
_____
_____
_____
_____
_____
_____
_____
_____

EPIC RANT

IN HINDSIGHT...
_____
_____
_____
_____
_____

SING IT!

WORD OF THE DAY

W S R E T O F

ALL *in* ALL,
A PRETTY
EPIC DAY!

EPIC METER

GENERAL NOTES

_____
_____
_____
_____
_____
_____
_____
_____

IN HINDSIGHT...

_____
_____
_____
_____
_____
_____
_____

ALL *in* ALL,
A PRETTY
EPIC DAY!

BREAKING NEWS

BULLETIN BOARD

LOST

WANTED

FOUND

TODAY, SUMMED UP IN PANTS

STAINED
SWEAT PANTS

SENSIBLE
SLACKS

Sexy leather *pants*

MESSAGE to the WORLD!

EPIC
METER

GENERAL NOTES

IN HINDSIGHT...

ALL in ALL,
A PRETTY
EPIC DAY!

Date: _____

EPIC METER

GENERAL NOTES

_____
_____
_____
_____
_____
_____
_____
_____
_____

IN HINDSIGHT...

_____
_____
_____
_____
_____
_____
_____
_____
_____

ALL *in* ALL,
A PRETTY
EPIC DAY!

MOOD FORECAST

WORLD'S BEST

_____

CURRENT KARAOKE JAM

TOMORROW'S PREDICTION

WRITE THE FIRST THING THAT POPS INTO YOUR HEAD.

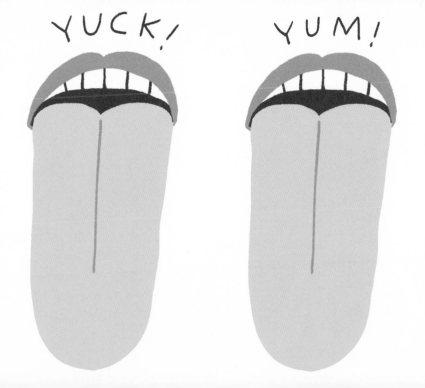

Date: _____

EPIC
METER

GENERAL NOTES

_____
_____
_____
_____
_____
_____
_____
_____

IN HINDSIGHT...

_____
_____
_____
_____
_____
_____
_____

ALL in ALL, A PRETTY EPIC DAY!

VENT HERE

_____ _____
_____ _____
_____ _____
_____ _____

ACCOMPLISHMENTS

MAJOR	MINOR	MEH

HOW CLOSE TO THE TARGET WERE YOU TODAY?

EPIC RANT

EVERYONE SHOULD...

Date:_____

EPIC METER

GENERAL NOTES

_____
_____
_____
_____
_____
_____
_____
_____
_____
_____
_____
_____
_____

IN HINDSIGHT...

_____
_____
_____
_____
_____
_____
_____
_____
_____
_____
_____

SPICE up THE DAY!

ALL in ALL, A PRETTY EPIC DAY!

EPIC

METER

GENERAL NOTES

_____
_____
_____
_____
_____
_____
_____
_____
_____
_____

IN HINDSIGHT...

_____
_____
_____
_____
_____
_____
_____
_____
_____
_____
_____

ALL in ALL, A PRETTY EPIC DAY!

EPIC RANT

Why do we STILL...

RANT OVER.

ADVICE COLUMN

FEELING STUMPED

IMMENSE PROBLEMS

EPIC  METER

GENERAL NOTES

_____
_____
_____
_____
_____
_____
_____
_____
_____

IN HINDSIGHT...

_____
_____
_____
_____
_____
_____
_____

ALL in ALL, A PRETTY EPIC DAY!

Date: _____

EPIC
METER

_____
_____
_____
_____
_____
_____
_____
_____

TODAY'S TAKEAWAY

Date: _____

EPIC
METER

_____
_____
_____
_____
_____
_____
_____
_____

Today's Lesson

TODAY'S TOP 10

10
9
8
7
6
5
4
3
2
1

PRO TIP:

CURRENT OBSESSION

what are we celebrating?

Date: _____

EPIC METER

GENERAL NOTES
_____
_____
_____
_____
_____
_____
_____

IN HINDSIGHT...
_____
_____
_____
_____
_____
_____

ALL in ALL, A PRETTY EPIC DAY!

EPIC
METER

GENERAL NOTES

_____
_____
_____
_____
_____
_____
_____
_____
_____
_____
_____
_____

IN HINDSIGHT...

_____
_____
_____
_____
_____
_____
_____
_____

ALL in ALL,
A PRETTY
EPIC DAY!

RETRACE your STEPS

START
1
2
3
4
5
6
7
END

DA BOMB or TODAY BOMBED IT?

CURRENT OBSESSION

BIG Announcement

WAS THE GLASS...
○ HALF-FULL?
○ HALF-EMPTY?
○ OVERFLOWING?
○ BONE-DRY?

Date: _____

EPIC METER

GENERAL NOTES
_____
_____
_____
_____
_____
_____
_____
_____
_____

IN HINDSIGHT...
_____
_____
_____
_____
_____
_____
_____
_____

ALL in ALL, A PRETTY EPIC DAY!

Date:_____

EPIC
METER

GENERAL NOTES
_____
_____
_____
_____
_____
_____
_____
_____
_____
_____

IN HINDSIGHT...
_____
_____
_____
_____
_____
_____
_____
_____

ALL *in* ALL,
A PRETTY
EPIC DAY!

HIGH POINTS of the DAY vs. LOW POINTS

WHAT WILL GO DOWN IN HISTORY TODAY

THIS SUCKS

_____

(BUT SOON IT WON'T)

CERTIFICATE OF
TODAY'S ACCOMPLISHMENTS

EPIC

METER

GENERAL NOTES

_____
_____
_____
_____
_____
_____
_____
_____
_____
_____
_____

IN HINDSIGHT...

_____
_____
_____
_____
_____
_____
_____
_____
_____
_____

ALL in ALL,
A PRETTY
EPIC DAY!

Date: _____

EPIC

METER

_____
_____
_____
_____
_____
_____
_____
_____

GOALS

Date: _____

EPIC

METER

_____
_____
_____
_____
_____
_____
_____
_____
_____
_____
_____

TODAY'S ODDITIES

A NEW PERSPECTIVE

Date:_____

EPIC METER

GENERAL NOTES

_____
_____
_____
_____
_____
_____
_____
_____
_____
_____

IN HINDSIGHT...

_____
_____
_____
_____
_____
_____
_____
_____
_____

ALL in ALL, A PRETTY EPIC DAY!

EPIC
METER

GENERAL NOTES

_____
_____
_____
_____
_____
_____
_____
_____

IN HINDSIGHT...

_____
_____
_____
_____
_____
_____

ALL *in* ALL,
A PRETTY
EPIC DAY!

SOMETHING YOU'VE BEEN MEANING TO GET OFF YOUR BACK:

when life hands you LEMONS, turn them INTO...

TODAY COULD'VE USED AN · · AUTOMATED · ·

01

Where WOULD you HEAD on the OPEN ROAD?

EPIC

METER

GENERAL NOTES

_____
_____
_____
_____
_____
_____
_____
_____
_____
_____
_____

IN HINDSIGHT...

_____
_____
_____
_____
_____
_____
_____
_____

ALL in ALL, A PRETTY EPIC DAY!

Date: _____

EPIC METER

GENERAL NOTES

_____
_____
_____
_____
_____
_____
_____
_____
_____

IN HINDSIGHT...

_____
_____
_____
_____
_____
_____
_____
_____

ALL in ALL, A PRETTY EPIC DAY!

WISH LIST

SH*T LIST

WHEN THE PLANETS ALIGN

_____
_____
_____
_____
_____

COUNT YOUR LUCKY STARS

Date:_____

EPIC

METER

_____
_____
_____
_____
_____
_____
_____
_____

SARDINES
JAM-PACKED DAY

Date:_____

EPIC

METER

_____
_____
_____
_____
_____
_____

EPIC METER

GENERAL NOTES

_____
_____
_____
_____
_____
_____
_____
_____
_____
_____
_____

IN HINDSIGHT...

_____
_____
_____
_____
_____
_____
_____
_____
_____

ALL in ALL, A PRETTY EPIC DAY!

JUST PUTTING THIS OUT THERE...

TODAY'S
TOP 10

10
9
8
7
6
5
4
3
2
1

PRO TIP:

CURRENT
OBSESSION

what are we celebrating?

EPIC
METER

GENERAL NOTES

_____
_____
_____
_____
_____
_____
_____

IN HINDSIGHT...

_____
_____
_____
_____
_____
_____

ALL in ALL,
A PRETTY
EPIC DAY!

EPIC

METER

GENERAL NOTES

_____
_____
_____
_____
_____
_____
_____
_____
_____
_____
_____

IN HINDSIGHT...

_____
_____
_____
_____
_____
_____
_____
_____

ALL in ALL,
A PRETTY
EPIC DAY!

NOTEWORTHY NEWS

_____
_____

HEY! WHAT'S COOKIN'?

WELL-DONE	HALF-BAKED	OVERDONE

ONCE in a Blue Moon

EPIC
METER

GENERAL NOTES

_____
_____
_____
_____
_____
_____
_____
_____
_____
_____
_____
_____
_____

IN HINDSIGHT...

_____
_____
_____
_____
_____
_____
_____
_____
_____
_____
_____

ALL in ALL,
A PRETTY
EPIC DAY!

Date: _____

EPIC METER

GENERAL NOTES

_____
_____
_____
_____
_____
_____
_____
_____
_____
_____
_____

IN HINDSIGHT...

_____
_____
_____
_____
_____
_____
_____
_____
_____

ALL in ALL, A PRETTY EPIC DAY!

FUTURE BUSINESSES

WHAT **HOOPS** DID YOU HAVE TO JUMP THROUGH TODAY?

BUDDING IDEAS

EPIC
METER

EPIC
METER

EXPRESS TICKET

TO: _____

_____

Date: _____

EPIC
METER

GENERAL NOTES
_____
_____
_____
_____
_____
_____
_____
_____
_____

IN HINDSIGHT...
_____
_____
_____
_____
_____
_____
_____
_____

ALL in ALL,
A PRETTY
EPIC DAY!

FRUITS of YOUR LABOR

WALL of FAME   WALL of SHAME

DEEP THOUGHTS

SHIPWRECKS

BURIED TREASURE

EPIC METER

GENERAL NOTES

_____
_____
_____
_____
_____
_____
_____
_____
_____
_____

IN HINDSIGHT...

_____
_____
_____
_____
_____
_____
_____

ALL in ALL, A PRETTY EPIC DAY!

Date:_____

EPIC

METER

GENERAL NOTES

_____
_____
_____
_____
_____
_____
_____
_____

IN HINDSIGHT...

_____
_____
_____
_____
_____
_____
_____

ALL in ALL, A PRETTY EPIC DAY!

STEPPING STONES

BUILDING BLOCKS

LOOKING FORWARD TO...

OFFICIAL COUNTDOWN

(YOUR MESSAGE HERE)

ORGANIZE YOUR THOUGHTS

EPIC METER

GENERAL NOTES

_____
_____
_____
_____
_____
_____
_____
_____
_____
_____

IN HINDSIGHT...

_____
_____
_____
_____
_____
_____
_____
_____

ALL *in* ALL,
A PRETTY
EPIC DAY!

Date: _____

EPIC
METER

_____
_____
_____
_____
_____
_____
_____
_____

SNAP DECISION
maker

#1 _____ #2 _____ #3 _____

NOPE   YASS!   NAH

Date: _____

EPIC
METER

_____
_____
_____
_____
_____
_____
_____

WHERE DID YOU GO?

WHO DID YOU SEE?

WHAT DO YOU KNOW?

The TITLE of TODAY'S BOOK   The TITLE of YESTERDAY'S BOOK   Date:_____

EPIC
METER

GENERAL NOTES
_____
_____
_____
_____
_____
_____
_____
_____
_____
_____
_____
_____

WHICH TOOL WILL REPAIR TODAY? (CIRCLE ONE)

IN HINDSIGHT...
_____
_____
_____
_____
_____
_____
_____
_____
_____

THE TUNNEL

THE LIGHT
at the END of IT

ALL in ALL,
A PRETTY
EPIC DAY!

Date:_____

EPIC
METER

GENERAL NOTES

_____
_____
_____
_____
_____
_____
_____
_____
_____
_____

IN HINDSIGHT...

_____
_____
_____
_____
_____
_____
_____
_____
_____

ALL in ALL, A PRETTY EPIC DAY!

Recipe for SUCCESS

Recipe for DISASTER

With a DASH of

and a PINCH of

ADD a TOUCH of

and TOP with

AIR YOUR GRIEVANCES

LIFE REPORT CARD

A-DOING GREAT	B-NOT BAD	C-NEEDS IMPROVEMENT	D-THAT DIDN'T GO WELL	F-UGHH!!

SUBJECT	GRADE

Extra Credit

EPIC METER

GENERAL NOTES

_____
_____
_____
_____
_____
_____
_____
_____
_____
_____

IN HINDSIGHT...

_____
_____
_____
_____
_____
_____
_____
_____
_____
_____

ALL *in* ALL,
A PRETTY
EPIC DAY!

Date: _____

EPIC

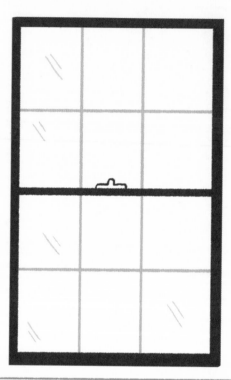

METER

GENERAL NOTES

_____
_____
_____
_____
_____
_____
_____

IN HINDSIGHT...

_____
_____
_____
_____
_____
_____
_____
_____
_____

ALL in ALL, A PRETTY EPIC DAY!

WINDOWS OF OPPORTUNITY

IT WAS THE BEST OF TIMES	IT WAS THE WORST OF TIMES

TODAY'S GOOD EGGS

TODAY'S BAD APPLES

Date: _____

EPIC METER

GENERAL NOTES

_____
_____
_____
_____
_____
_____
_____
_____
_____

IN HINDSIGHT...

_____
_____
_____
_____
_____
_____
_____
_____
_____

ALL in ALL,
A PRETTY
EPIC DAY!

Date: _____

EPIC METER

GENERAL NOTES

_____
_____
_____
_____
_____
_____
_____
_____
_____

IN HINDSIGHT...

_____
_____
_____
_____
_____
_____
_____

ALL in ALL, A PRETTY EPIC DAY!

WHAT YOU SAID:

WHAT YOU ACTUALLY wanted TO SAY:

WHAT YOU MEANT TO SAY:

HIGH NOTES

HARMONY

LOW NOTES

Let it SOAK in...

Date: _____

EPIC METER

GENERAL NOTES

_____
_____
_____
_____
_____
_____
_____
_____
_____
_____
_____
_____
_____

IN HINDSIGHT...

_____
_____
_____
_____
_____
_____
_____
_____
_____

ALL in ALL, A PRETTY EPIC DAY!

Date: _____

RETRACE your STEPS

EPIC METER

GENERAL NOTES

_____
_____
_____
_____
_____
_____
_____
_____
_____
_____
_____

IN HINDSIGHT...

_____
_____
_____
_____
_____
_____
_____
_____

ALL in ALL, A PRETTY EPIC DAY!

GROCERY

$1

Café

BOOKS

BAKERY

your message here ↴

EPIC
METER

GENERAL NOTES
_____
_____
_____
_____
_____
_____
_____

IN HINDSIGHT...
_____
_____
_____
_____
_____
_____

ALL *in* ALL,
A PRETTY
EPIC DAY!

IRON OUT the DETAILS

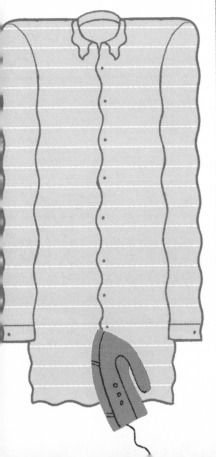

WORK OUT the KINKS

Date: _____

EPIC METER

GENERAL NOTES
_____
_____
_____
_____
_____
_____
_____
_____

IN HINDSIGHT...
_____
_____
_____
_____
_____
_____
_____
_____
_____

ALL *in* ALL, A PRETTY EPIC DAY!

MAJOR GROWTH

_____
_____
_____
_____
_____
_____

SEEDLINGS

_____
_____
_____
_____
_____
_____

UP FOR A CELEBRATORY HAND GESTURE (CIRCLE ON

High 5

Low 5

Too Slow

SHED LIGHT ON the SITUATION

EPIC RANT

What is going on with...

_____
_____
_____
_____
_____
_____
_____
_____
_____
_____
_____
_____
_____
_____
_____
_____
_____
_____
_____
_____
_____
_____
_____
_____
_____

EPIC METER

GENERAL NOTES

_____
_____
_____
_____
_____
_____
_____
_____
_____

IN HINDSIGHT...

_____
_____
_____
_____
_____
_____

ALL in ALL, A PRETTY EPIC DAY!

Date: _____

EPIC METER

_____
_____
_____
_____
_____
_____
_____
_____

TODAY'S TAKEAWAY

Date: _____

EPIC METER

_____
_____
_____
_____
_____
_____
_____

Today's Lesson

Date: _____

EPIC METER

GENERAL NOTES
_____
_____
_____
_____
_____
_____
_____
_____
_____

IN HINDSIGHT...
_____
_____
_____
_____
_____
_____
_____

ALL *in* ALL, A PRETTY EPIC DAY!

EPIC

METER

GENERAL NOTES

_____
_____
_____
_____
_____
_____
_____

IN HINDSIGHT...

_____
_____
_____
_____
_____
_____

ALL *in* ALL, A PRETTY EPIC DAY!

The ULTIMATE DECISION

PROS	CONS

WHAT'S THE VERDICT?

SATISFIED WITH THE OUTCOME? YES or N[O]

RECORD A **VICTORY**,

ou accomplished enough today!

TODAY WERE YOU SWITCHED ON or OFF?

HOW DIFFICULT WAS IT TO GET FROM POINT (A) to POINT (B) TODAY?

A

B

TAKE a CLOSER LOOK

EPIC METER

GENERAL NOTES

IN HINDSIGHT...

ALL in ALL, A PRETTY EPIC DAY!

Date:_____

EPIC METER

GENERAL NOTES

_____
_____
_____
_____
_____
_____
_____
_____
_____

IN HINDSIGHT...

_____
_____
_____
_____
_____
_____
_____
_____

ALL in ALL, A PRETTY EPIC DAY!

HOW FAR DID YOU GET CONQUERING THE DAY?

YAY!

NEARLY THERE...

STARTING is HALF the BATTLE

TODAY'S CHECKLIST

- ◎ GOT STUFF DONE
- ◎ LAUGHED
- ◎ WAS HELPFUL
- ◎ ATE SOMETHING
- ◎ HAD FUN

The
KEY
to
TODAY'S

SUCCESS

BRIGHT IDEAS

EPIC

METER

GENERAL NOTES

_____
_____
_____
_____
_____
_____
_____
_____
_____
_____
_____

IN HINDSIGHT...

_____
_____
_____
_____
_____
_____
_____
_____

ALL in ALL,
A PRETTY
EPIC DAY!

Date:_____

EPIC
METER

_____
_____
_____
_____
_____
_____
_____

SNAP DECISION
maker

#1 [_____] #2 [_____] #3 [_____]

NOPE   YASS!   NAH

Date:_____

EPIC
METER

_____
_____
_____
_____
_____
_____
_____

WHERE DID YOU GO?

WHO DID YOU SEE?

WHAT DO YOU KNOW?

What's the SCOOP?

LET IT SIMMER HERE...

EPIC METER

GENERAL NOTES

_____
_____
_____
_____
_____
_____
_____
_____
_____

IN HINDSIGHT...

_____
_____
_____
_____
_____
_____

ALL in ALL, A PRETTY EPIC DAY!

Date: _____

GENERAL NOTES

_____
_____
_____
_____
_____
_____
_____
_____
_____
_____

IN HINDSIGHT...

_____
_____
_____
_____
_____
_____
_____
_____

ALL in ALL,
A PRETTY
EPIC DAY!

WHAT WOULD YOU STITCH ON YOUR JEAN JACKET?

FREE WISH

EPIC METER

GENERAL NOTES

_____
_____
_____
_____
_____
_____
_____
_____
_____
_____
_____
_____
_____
_____

IN HINDSIGHT...

_____
_____
_____
_____
_____
_____
_____

ALL in ALL, A PRETTY EPIC DAY!

Hear ye, Hear ye!

IMPORTANT ANNOUNCEMENT!

REQUEST FORM
═ OFFICIAL DO-OVER REQUEST ═

REASON:

_____
_____
_____

Date:_____

EPIC
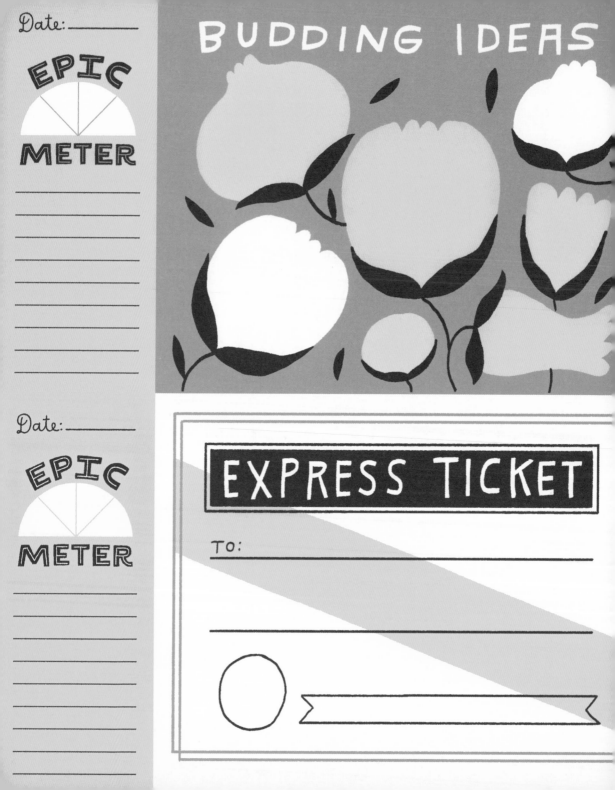
METER

_____
_____
_____
_____
_____
_____
_____
_____

Date:_____

EPIC
METER

_____
_____
_____
_____
_____
_____
_____

BUDDING IDEAS

EXPRESS TICKET

TO: _____

_____

A GOOD TIME to Reflect

Date:‌_____

EPIC METER

GENERAL NOTES

IN HINDSIGHT...

ALL in ALL, A PRETTY EPIC DAY!

Date: _____

EPIC
METER

GENERAL NOTES
_____
_____
_____
_____
_____
_____
_____
_____
_____
_____
_____

IN HINDSIGHT...
_____
_____
_____
_____
_____
_____
_____

**ALL in ALL,
A PRETTY
EPIC DAY!**

CURRENT MOOD

JUST *it*
YELL OUT!

HOW DID TODAY
MEASURE UP

TODAY   YESTERDA

PRO
TIP:

EPIC

METER

GENERAL NOTES

_____
_____
_____
_____
_____
_____
_____
_____
_____
_____
_____
_____

IN HINDSIGHT...

_____
_____
_____
_____
_____
_____
_____
_____

ALL in ALL,
A PRETTY
EPIC DAY!

Date: _____

EPIC METER

GENERAL NOTES

_____
_____
_____
_____
_____
_____
_____
_____

IN HINDSIGHT...

_____
_____
_____
_____
_____
_____
_____

ALL in ALL, A PRETTY EPIC DAY!

HOW IS IT POSSIBLE...

_____
_____
_____
_____
_____
_____
_____
_____
_____
_____
_____
_____
_____
_____
_____
_____
_____

Rant Over.

ON SECOND THOUGHT...

_____
_____
_____
_____
_____
_____
_____

CURRENT DAYDREAMS

IT HAS BEEN

DAYS SINCE THE LAST HAPPY ACCIDENT.

IT'S in the BAG!

EPIC

METER

GENERAL NOTES

_____
_____
_____
_____

_____
_____
_____

IN HINDSIGHT...

_____
_____
_____
_____
_____
_____

CURRENT OBSESSION

ALL in ALL, A PRETTY EPIC DAY!

Date: _____

EPIC METER

GENERAL NOTES

_____
_____
_____
_____
_____
_____
_____
_____

IN HINDSIGHT...

_____
_____
_____
_____
_____
_____
_____

ALL *in* ALL, A PRETTY EPIC DAY!

CAUTION

AHEAD

OVERHEAR *anything* INTERESTING TODAY?

INTERESTING OBSERVATION

GROUNDBREAKING DISCOVERY

FILL 'ER UP!

EPIC METER

ONE STEP at a TIME

EPIC METER

Date: _____

EPIC METER

GENERAL NOTES

_____
_____
_____
_____
_____
_____
_____
_____
_____

IN HINDSIGHT...

_____
_____
_____
_____
_____
_____
_____

ALL *in* ALL, A PRETTY EPIC DAY!

Once Upon Today

_____
_____
_____
_____
_____
_____
_____
_____
_____
_____
_____
_____
_____
_____
_____
_____
_____
_____
_____
_____
_____
_____
_____
_____
_____

The End

TODAY'S HEADLINE

EPIC DAILY

3 WISHES

FRIENDS *you're* ROOTING *for*

EPIC METER

GENERAL NOTES

_____
_____
_____
_____
_____
_____
_____
_____
_____
_____

IN HINDSIGHT...

_____
_____
_____
_____
_____
_____
_____
_____
_____
_____

ALL *in* ALL, A PRETTY EPIC DAY!

EPIC
METER

GENERAL NOTES

_____
_____
_____
_____
_____
_____
_____
_____
_____

IN HINDSIGHT...

_____
_____
_____
_____
_____
_____
_____
_____

ALL *in* ALL,
A PRETTY
EPIC DAY!

BIG PLANS

WRITE IT DOWN

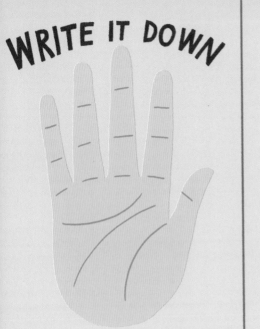

BEFORE YOU FORGET

LEFTOVER PROBLEMS

EPIC

METER

GENERAL NOTES

_____
_____
_____
_____
_____
_____
_____

IN HINDSIGHT...

_____
_____
_____
_____
_____
_____
_____
_____
_____

ALL in ALL, A PRETTY EPIC DAY!

FILL ANY BIG SHOES TODAY?

OR SMELLY SOCKS?

OR BARE FEET?

OR COWBOY BOOTS?

Date: _____

EPIC METER

_____
_____
_____
_____
_____
_____
_____
_____

WHAT YOU SAID:

WHAT YOU ACTUALLY wanted TO SAY:

WHAT YOU MEANT TO SAY:

Date: _____

EPIC METER

_____
_____
_____
_____
_____
_____

HIGH NOTES

HARMONY

LOW NOTES

LADDER to SUCCESS

EPIC METER

GENERAL NOTES

_____
_____
_____
_____
_____
_____
_____
_____
_____
_____

IN HINDSIGHT...

_____
_____
_____
_____
_____
_____
_____
_____
_____

ALL in ALL,
A PRETTY
EPIC DAY!

Date:_____

EPIC METER

GENERAL NOTES

_____
_____
_____
_____
_____
_____
_____

IN HINDSIGHT...

_____
_____
_____
_____
_____
_____

ALL *in* ALL, A PRETTY EPIC DAY!

SPECIAL REMINDER

UPON FURTHER INVESTIGATION

SUBJECT:

EXPLANATION

The RESULT

Could this day get any SWEETER?

_____
_____
_____
_____

Sugar NEEDS ___ more SPOONFULS

Random Act of Kindness

CAUSES WORTH ROOTING FOR

EPIC METER

GENERAL NOTES

_____
_____
_____
_____
_____
_____
_____
_____
_____
_____

IN HINDSIGHT...

_____
_____
_____
_____
_____
_____
_____
_____

ALL in ALL, A PRETTY EPIC DAY!

Date: _____

EPIC

METER

GENERAL NOTES

_____
_____
_____
_____
_____
_____
_____
_____
_____

IN HINDSIGHT...

_____
_____
_____
_____
_____
_____
_____
_____

ALL in ALL, A PRETTY EPIC DAY!

EPIC RANT

REALLY?! REALLY.

RANT OVER.

SPECIAL KEEPSAKE

NAME THIS CAT

_____

Date: _____

EPIC METER

GENERAL NOTES

_____
_____
_____
_____
_____
_____
_____
_____

TEMS THAT ARE STILL LOST

MYSTERIOUSLY MISSING↗

NEVER LENDING MY STUFF AGAIN...

↖MISS that ONE...

↖WHERE COULD IT BE?!

WHY?

HMM...

IN HINDSIGHT...

_____
_____
_____
_____
_____
_____
_____

NOW THAT'S A REASON TO CELEBRATE!

ALL in ALL, A PRETTY EPIC DAY!

EPIC
METER

_____
_____
_____
_____
_____
_____
_____
_____

GOALS

EPIC
METER

_____
_____
_____
_____
_____
_____
_____

TODAY'S ODDITIES

Let it SOAK in...

EPIC METER

GENERAL NOTES

_____
_____
_____
_____
_____
_____
_____
_____

IN HINDSIGHT...

_____
_____
_____
_____
_____
_____
_____

ALL in ALL, A PRETTY EPIC DAY!

Date: _____

EPIC METER

GENERAL NOTES
_____
_____
_____
_____
_____
_____
_____
_____
_____
_____

IN HINDSIGHT...
_____
_____
_____
_____
_____
_____
_____
_____

ALL in ALL, A PRETTY EPIC DAY!

TODAY'S ACCOMPLISHMENTS

PROBLEM-REPAIR-SHOP QUEUE
_____
_____
_____
_____
_____
_____

Nothing is unfixable!

TRY to WALK in SOMEONE ELSE'S SHOES

Learn anything on the journey?

_____
_____
_____
_____

HOW did TODAY START?

HOW did TODAY END?

IS EVERYTHING ORGANIZED?

EPIC METER

GENERAL NOTES

_____
_____
_____
_____
_____
_____
_____
_____
_____

IN HINDSIGHT...

_____
_____
_____
_____
_____
_____
_____
_____

ALL in ALL, A PRETTY EPIC DAY!

Date: _____

EPIC METER

GENERAL NOTES

_____
_____
_____
_____
_____
_____
_____
_____

IN HINDSIGHT...

_____
_____
_____
_____
_____
_____
_____

ALL in ALL, A PRETTY EPIC DAY!

LIE AWAKE THINKING

Fond Memory

TODAY'S LOG

COUNT YOUR LUCKY STARS

Date: _____

EPIC
METER

Date: _____

EPIC
METER

SARDINES JAM-PACKED DAY

Date:_____

EPIC
METER

GENERAL NOTES

_____
_____
_____
_____
_____
_____
_____
_____

IN HINDSIGHT...

_____
_____
_____
_____
_____
_____

ALL in ALL, A PRETTY EPIC DAY!

PERFORMANCE ★ RANKING ★

_____ ROOKIE

_____ NOVICE

_____ EXPERT

_____ VETERAN

_____ GRIZZLED

HATS OFF TO YOU

Today's Specials

YOUR 2¢

Greetings from... · SUNNY · RAINY · BORING · EXPENSIVE

_____

WHERE I LEARNED THAT...

_____

EPIC METER

EPIC RANT

GENERAL NOTES

_____
_____
_____
_____
_____
_____
_____
_____
_____
_____

IN HINDSIGHT...

_____
_____
_____
_____

SING IT!

WORD OF THE DAY

ALL *in* ALL, A PRETTY EPIC DAY!

Date: _____

EPIC METER

GENERAL NOTES
_____
_____
_____
_____
_____
_____
_____
_____
_____

IN HINDSIGHT...
_____
_____
_____
_____
_____
_____
_____
_____
_____

ALL in ALL,
A PRETTY
EPIC DAY!

BREAKING NEWS

BULLETIN BOARD

LOST

WANTED

FOUND

TODAY, SUMMED UP IN PANTS

STAINED
SWEATPANTS

SENSIBLE
SLACKS

Sexy
leather
pants

MESSAGE to the WORLD!

EPIC

METER

GENERAL NOTES

_____
_____
_____
_____
_____
_____
_____
_____
_____

IN HINDSIGHT...

_____
_____
_____
_____
_____
_____
_____

ALL *in* ALL,
A PRETTY
EPIC DAY!

Date: _____

EPIC
METER

GENERAL NOTES
_____
_____
_____
_____
_____
_____
_____
_____

IN HINDSIGHT...
_____
_____
_____
_____
_____
_____
_____
_____

ALL *in* ALL,
A PRETTY
EPIC DAY!

MOOD
FORECAST

WORLD'S
BEST
_____

CURRENT
KARAOKE JAM
_____

TOMORROW'S
PREDICTION

WRITE THE FIRST THING THAT POPS INTO YOUR HEAD.

YUCK! YUM!

Date:_____

EPIC METER

GENERAL NOTES

_____
_____
_____
_____
_____
_____
_____
_____
_____

IN HINDSIGHT...

_____
_____
_____
_____
_____
_____

ALL *in* ALL,
A PRETTY
EPIC DAY!

VENT HERE

_____
_____
_____
_____
_____

ACCOMPLISHMENTS

MAJOR	MINOR	MEH

HOW CLOSE TO **THE TARGET** WERE YOU TODAY?

EVERYONE SHOULD...

SPICE up THE DAY!

Date:_____

EPIC METER

GENERAL NOTES
_____
_____
_____
_____
_____
_____
_____
_____
_____
_____
_____
_____

IN HINDSIGHT...
_____
_____
_____
_____
_____
_____
_____
_____
_____

ALL in ALL, A PRETTY EPIC DAY!

Date: _____

EPIC

METER

GENERAL NOTES

_____
_____
_____
_____
_____
_____
_____
_____
_____
_____
_____

IN HINDSIGHT...

_____
_____
_____
_____
_____
_____
_____
_____

ALL in ALL, A PRETTY EPIC DAY!

EPIC RANT

Why do we STILL...

RANT OVER.

ADVICE COLUMN

FEELING STUMPED

EPIC METER

GENERAL NOTES

_____
_____
_____
_____
_____
_____
_____

IMMENSE PROBLEMS

IN HINDSIGHT...

_____
_____
_____
_____
_____
_____
_____
_____

ALL in ALL, A PRETTY EPIC DAY!

Date:_____

EPIC
METER

_____
_____
_____
_____
_____
_____
_____
_____

TODAY'S TAKEAWAY

Date:_____

EPIC
METER

_____
_____
_____
_____
_____
_____
_____

Today's Lesson

TODAY'S
TOP 10

10
9
8
7
6
5
4
3
2
1

PRO TIP:

CURRENT OBSESSION

Date: _____

EPIC METER

GENERAL NOTES
_____
_____
_____
_____
_____
_____
_____
_____
_____
_____

IN HINDSIGHT...
_____
_____
_____
_____
_____
_____
_____
_____
_____
_____
_____

ALL in ALL, A PRETTY EPIC DAY!

what are we celebrating?

Date: _____

EPIC
METER

GENERAL NOTES

_____
_____
_____
_____
_____
_____
_____
_____
_____

IN HINDSIGHT...

_____
_____
_____
_____
_____
_____
_____
_____

ALL in ALL,
A PRETTY
EPIC DAY!

RETRACE your STEPS

START

1

2

3

4

5

6

7

END

DA BOMB or

TODAY

BOMBED IT?

CURRENT OBSESSION

EPIC

METER

GENERAL NOTES

_____
_____
_____
_____
_____
_____
_____
_____
_____

IN HINDSIGHT...

_____
_____
_____
_____
_____
_____
_____

BIG Announcement

WAS THE GLASS...
- HALF-FULL?
- HALF-EMPTY?
- OVERFLOWING?
- BONE-DRY?

ALL in ALL, A PRETTY EPIC DAY!

Date:_____

EPIC METER

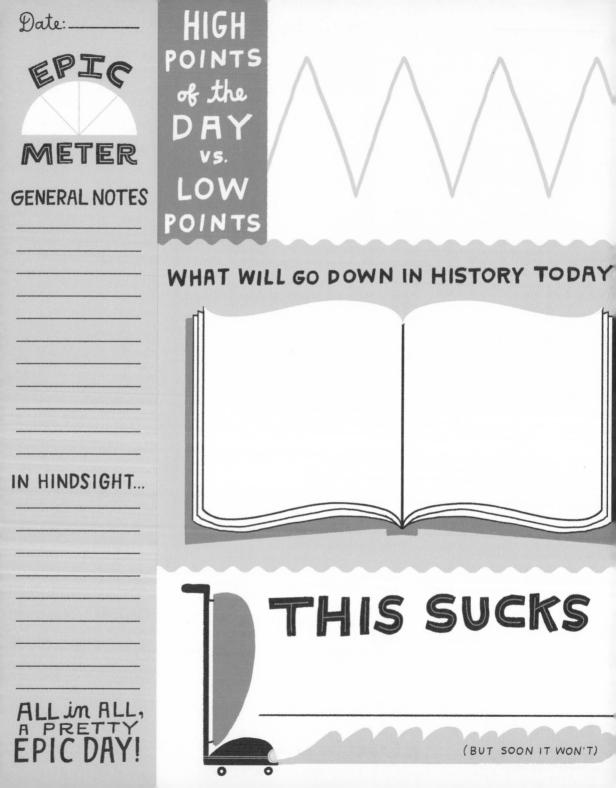

GENERAL NOTES

_____
_____
_____
_____
_____
_____
_____
_____
_____

IN HINDSIGHT...

_____
_____
_____
_____
_____
_____
_____
_____

ALL in ALL, A PRETTY EPIC DAY!

HIGH POINTS of the DAY vs. LOW POINTS

WHAT WILL GO DOWN IN HISTORY TODAY

THIS SUCKS

_____

(BUT SOON IT WON'T)

CERTIFICATE OF TODAY'S ACCOMPLISHMENTS

EPIC METER

GENERAL NOTES

_____
_____
_____
_____
_____
_____
_____
_____
_____
_____

IN HINDSIGHT...

_____
_____
_____
_____
_____
_____
_____
_____

ALL in ALL, A PRETTY EPIC DAY!

EPIC

METER

_____
_____
_____
_____
_____
_____
_____
_____

GOALS

EPIC

METER

_____
_____
_____
_____
_____
_____
_____
_____

TODAY'S ODDITIES

A NEW PERSPECTIVE

EPIC METER

GENERAL NOTES

_____
_____
_____
_____
_____
_____
_____

IN HINDSIGHT...

_____
_____
_____
_____
_____
_____
_____
_____

ALL *in* ALL, A PRETTY EPIC DAY!

EPIC METER

GENERAL NOTES

_____
_____
_____
_____
_____
_____
_____
_____
_____

IN HINDSIGHT...

_____
_____
_____
_____
_____
_____
_____

ALL in ALL, A PRETTY EPIC DAY!

SOMETHING YOU'VE BEEN MEANING TO GET OFF YOUR BACK:

when life hands you LEMONS, turn them INTO...

TODAY COULD'VE USED AN AUTOMATED

01

Where WOULD you HEAD on the OPEN ROAD?

EPIC METER

GENERAL NOTES

_____
_____
_____
_____
_____
_____
_____
_____
_____
_____

IN HINDSIGHT...

_____
_____
_____
_____
_____
_____
_____
_____
_____

ALL in ALL, A PRETTY EPIC DAY!

Date:_____

EPIC METER

GENERAL NOTES

_____
_____
_____
_____
_____
_____
_____
_____

IN HINDSIGHT...

_____
_____
_____
_____
_____
_____
_____
_____

ALL *in* ALL,
A PRETTY
EPIC DAY!

WISH LIST

SH✳T LIST

WHEN THE PLANETS ALIGN

_____
_____
_____
_____
_____

COUNT YOUR LUCKY STARS

EPIC
METER

_____
_____
_____
_____
_____
_____
_____

SARDINES
JAM-PACKED DAY

Date:_____

EPIC
METER

_____
_____
_____
_____
_____
_____
_____

Date: _____

EPIC METER

GENERAL NOTES

_____
_____
_____
_____
_____
_____
_____
_____
_____
_____

IN HINDSIGHT...

_____
_____
_____
_____
_____
_____
_____

ALL *in* ALL,
A PRETTY
EPIC DAY!

JUST PUTTING THIS OUT THERE...

TODAY'S
TOP 10

10
9
8
7
6
5
4
3
2
1

PRO TIP:

CURRENT OBSESSION

EPIC METER

GENERAL NOTES

IN HINDSIGHT...

what are we celebrating?

ALL in ALL, A PRETTY EPIC DAY!

EPIC

METER

GENERAL NOTES

IN HINDSIGHT...

ALL in ALL,
A PRETTY
EPIC DAY!

NOTEWORTHY NEWS

HEY! WHAT'S COOKIN'?

WELL-DONE	HALF-BAKED	OVERDONE

ONCE in a Blue Moon

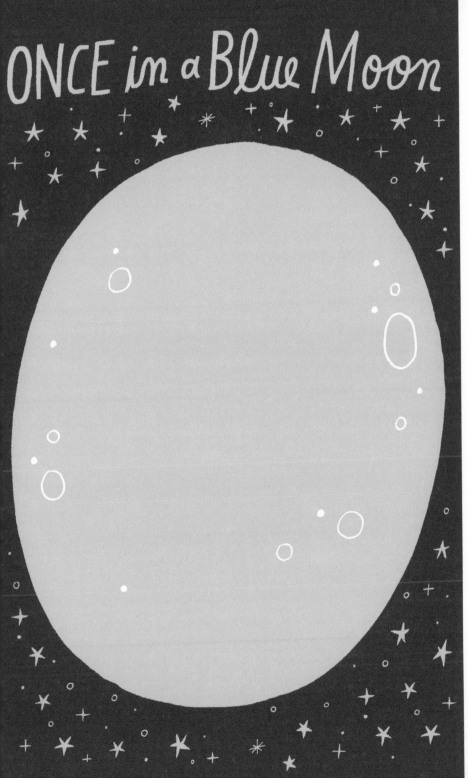

EPIC METER

GENERAL NOTES

_____
_____
_____
_____
_____
_____
_____
_____
_____

IN HINDSIGHT...

_____
_____
_____
_____
_____
_____
_____
_____

ALL in ALL, A PRETTY EPIC DAY!

Date:_____

EPIC
METER

GENERAL NOTES

_____
_____
_____
_____
_____
_____
_____
_____

IN HINDSIGHT...

_____
_____
_____
_____
_____
_____
_____
_____
_____

ALL in ALL,
A PRETTY
EPIC DAY!

FUTURE BUSINESSES

WHAT **HOOPS** DID YOU HAVE TO JUMP
THROUGH TODAY?

BUDDING IDEAS

EPIC

METER

_____
_____
_____
_____
_____
_____
_____
_____

EXPRESS TICKET

TO:_____

_____

EPIC

METER

_____
_____
_____
_____
_____
_____
_____
_____
_____

Date:_____

EPIC METER

GENERAL NOTES

_____
_____
_____
_____
_____
_____
_____
_____
_____
_____

IN HINDSIGHT...

_____
_____
_____
_____
_____
_____
_____
_____

ALL in ALL, A PRETTY EPIC DAY!

FRUITS of YOUR LABOR

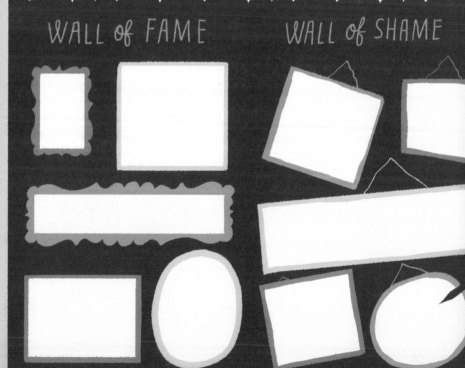

WALL of FAME   WALL of SHAME

DEEP THOUGHTS

SHIPWRECKS   BURIED TREASURE

Date: _____

EPIC METER

GENERAL NOTES
_____
_____
_____
_____
_____
_____
_____
_____
_____

IN HINDSIGHT...
_____
_____
_____
_____
_____
_____
_____

ALL *in* ALL, A PRETTY EPIC DAY!

Date:——————

EPIC METER

GENERAL NOTES

_____
_____
_____
_____
_____
_____
_____
_____
_____

IN HINDSIGHT...

_____
_____
_____
_____
_____
_____

ALL in ALL,
A PRETTY
EPIC DAY!

STEPPING STONES

BUILDING BLOCKS

LOOKING FORWARD TO...

OFFICIAL COUNTDOWN

(YOUR MESSAGE HERE)

ORGANIZE YOUR THOUGHTS

EPIC METER

GENERAL NOTES

_____
_____
_____
_____
_____
_____
_____
_____
_____
_____

IN HINDSIGHT...

_____
_____
_____
_____
_____
_____
_____
_____

ALL in ALL, A PRETTY EPIC DAY!

Date:_____

EPIC METER

_____
_____
_____
_____
_____
_____
_____

SNAP DECISION *maker*

#1 [_____]   #2 [_____]   #3 [_____]

[NOPE]   [YASS!]   [NAH]

Date:_____

EPIC METER

_____
_____
_____
_____
_____
_____
_____

WHERE DID YOU GO?

WHO DID YOU SEE?

WHAT DO YOU KNOW?

The TITLE of TODAY'S BOOK   The TITLE of YESTERDAY'S BOOK   Date:_____

EPIC METER

GENERAL NOTES

_____
_____
_____
_____
_____
_____
_____
_____
_____

WHICH TOOL WILL REPAIR TODAY? (CIRCLE ONE)

IN HINDSIGHT...

_____
_____
_____
_____
_____
_____

THE TUNNEL

THE LIGHT at the END of IT

ALL in ALL, A PRETTY EPIC DAY!

Date: _____

EPIC METER

GENERAL NOTES

_____
_____
_____
_____
_____
_____
_____
_____

IN HINDSIGHT...

_____
_____
_____
_____
_____
_____
_____
_____

ALL in ALL, A PRETTY EPIC DAY!

Recipe for SUCCESS

Recipe for DISASTER

With a DASH of

and a PINCH of

ADD a TOUCH of

and TOP with

AIR YOUR GRIEVANCES

LIFE REPORT CARD

A-DOING GREAT B-NOT BAD C-NEEDS IMPROVEMENT D-THAT DIDN'T GO WELL F-UGHH!!

SUBJECT	GRADE

Extra Credit

EPIC METER

GENERAL NOTES

_____
_____
_____
_____
_____
_____
_____
_____
_____
_____
_____
_____

IN HINDSIGHT...

_____
_____
_____
_____
_____
_____
_____
_____
_____
_____
_____
_____

ALL in ALL, A PRETTY EPIC DAY!

Date: _____

EPIC

METER

GENERAL NOTES

_____
_____
_____
_____
_____
_____
_____

IN HINDSIGHT...

_____
_____
_____
_____
_____
_____
_____

ALL in ALL, A PRETTY EPIC DAY!

WINDOWS OF OPPORTUNITY

IT WAS THE BEST OF TIMES	IT WAS THE WORST OF TIMES

TODAY'S GOOD EGGS

TODAY'S BAD APPLES

Date:_____

EPIC METER

GENERAL NOTES

_____
_____
_____
_____
_____
_____
_____

IN HINDSIGHT...

_____
_____
_____
_____
_____
_____
_____
_____

ALL *in* ALL,
A PRETTY
EPIC DAY!

Date: _____

EPIC
METER

_____
_____
_____
_____
_____
_____
_____
_____

WHAT YOU SAID:

WHAT YOU ACTUALLY
wanted TO SAY:

WHAT YOU MEANT TO SAY:

Date: _____

EPIC
METER

_____
_____
_____
_____
_____
_____
_____

HIGH NOTES

HARMONY

LOW NOTES

Let it SOAK in...

EPIC METER

GENERAL NOTES

_____
_____
_____
_____
_____
_____
_____
_____
_____
_____

IN HINDSIGHT...

_____
_____
_____
_____
_____
_____
_____

ALL in ALL, A PRETTY EPIC DAY!

Date: _____

EPIC METER

GENERAL NOTES

_____
_____
_____
_____
_____
_____
_____
_____
_____

IN HINDSIGHT...

_____
_____
_____
_____
_____
_____
_____

ALL in ALL, A PRETTY EPIC DAY!

RETRACE your STEPS

your message here ↴

EPIC

METER

GENERAL NOTES

IRON OUT the DETAILS

WORK OUT the KINKS

IN HINDSIGHT...

ALL *in* ALL, A PRETTY EPIC DAY!

Date: _____

EPIC METER

GENERAL NOTES

_____
_____
_____
_____
_____
_____
_____

IN HINDSIGHT...

_____
_____
_____
_____
_____
_____
_____
_____

ALL *in* ALL, A PRETTY EPIC DAY!

MAJOR GROWTH

_____
_____
_____
_____
_____

SEEDLINGS

_____
_____
_____
_____
_____
_____
_____

SHED LIGHT ON the SITUATION

UP FOR A CELEBRATORY HAND GESTURE (CIRCLE ONE)

High 5

Low 5

Too Slow

EPIC RANT

What is going on with...

_____
_____
_____
_____
_____
_____
_____
_____
_____
_____
_____
_____
_____
_____
_____
_____
_____
_____
_____
_____
_____
_____
_____
_____
_____

Date:_____

EPIC METER

GENERAL NOTES

_____
_____
_____
_____
_____
_____
_____

IN HINDSIGHT...

_____
_____
_____
_____
_____
_____

ALL in ALL, A PRETTY EPIC DAY!

Date: _____

EPIC
METER

_____
_____
_____
_____
_____
_____
_____
_____

TODAY'S TAKEAWAY

Date: _____

EPIC
METER

_____
_____
_____
_____
_____
_____
_____

Today's Lesson

How about these apples?

Date:_____

EPIC METER

GENERAL NOTES

_____
_____
_____
_____
_____
_____
_____
_____
_____
_____
_____

IN HINDSIGHT...

_____
_____
_____
_____
_____
_____
_____
_____

ALL in ALL, A PRETTY EPIC DAY!

Date: _____

EPIC METER

GENERAL NOTES

_____
_____
_____
_____
_____
_____
_____
_____
_____
_____

IN HINDSIGHT...

_____
_____
_____
_____
_____
_____
_____
_____
_____

ALL *in* ALL,
A PRETTY
EPIC DAY!

The ULTIMATE DECISION

PROS	CONS

WHAT'S THE VERDICT?

SATISFIED WITH THE OUTCOME? YES or NO

RECORD A VICTORY

You accomplished enough today!

TODAY WERE YOU SWITCHED ON or OFF?

HOW DIFFICULT WAS IT TO GET FROM POINT Ⓐ to POINT Ⓑ TODAY?

A
.

B
.

TAKE a CLOSER LOOK

Date:_____

EPIC METER

GENERAL NOTES

IN HINDSIGHT...

ALL in ALL, A PRETTY EPIC DAY!

Date:_____

EPIC
METER

GENERAL NOTES

_____
_____
_____
_____
_____
_____
_____
_____
_____

IN HINDSIGHT...

_____
_____
_____
_____
_____
_____

ALL in ALL, A PRETTY EPIC DAY!

HOW FAR DID YOU GET CONQUERING THE DAY?

YAY!

NEARLY THERE...

STARTING is HALF the BATTLE

TODAY'S CHECKLIST

○ GOT STUFF DONE

○ LAUGHED

○ WAS HELPFUL

○ ATE SOMETHING

○ HAD FUN

The KEY to TODAY'S SUCCESS

BRIGHT IDEAS

EPIC

METER

GENERAL NOTES

_____
_____
_____
_____
_____
_____
_____
_____
_____
_____

IN HINDSIGHT...

_____
_____
_____
_____
_____
_____
_____
_____

ALL in ALL,
A PRETTY
EPIC DAY!

Date:_____

EPIC METER

_____
_____
_____
_____
_____
_____
_____
_____
_____

SNAP DECISION
maker

#1 _____ #2 _____ #3 _____

NOPE   YASS!   NAH

Date:_____

EPIC METER

_____
_____
_____
_____
_____
_____
_____

WHERE DID YOU GO?

WHO DID YOU SEE?

WHAT DO YOU KNOW?

WHAT'S THE SCOOP?

LET IT SIMMER HERE...

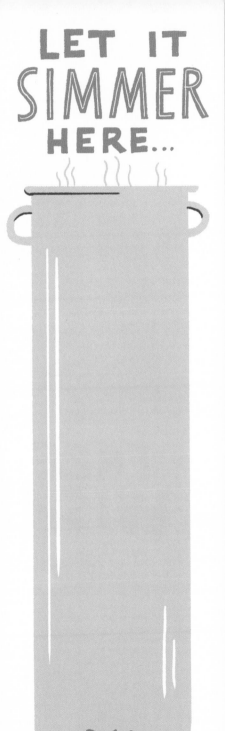

EPIC METER

GENERAL NOTES

_____
_____
_____
_____
_____
_____
_____
_____
_____

IN HINDSIGHT...

_____
_____
_____
_____
_____
_____
_____
_____

ALL in ALL, A PRETTY EPIC DAY!

Date: _____

GENERAL NOTES

_____
_____
_____
_____
_____
_____
_____
_____

IN HINDSIGHT...

_____
_____
_____
_____
_____
_____
_____

ALL in ALL,
A PRETTY
EPIC DAY!

WHAT WOULD YOU STITCH ON YOUR JEAN JACKET?

FREE WISH

IMPORTANT ANNOUNCEMENT!

REQUEST FORM
OFFICIAL DO-OVER REQUEST

REASON:

EPIC METER

GENERAL NOTES

IN HINDSIGHT...

ALL in ALL, A PRETTY EPIC DAY!

EPIC

METER

_____
_____
_____
_____
_____
_____
_____
_____

BUDDING IDEAS

EPIC

METER

_____
_____
_____
_____
_____
_____
_____
_____

EXPRESS TICKET

TO: _____

_____

A GOOD TIME to Reflect

EPIC METER

GENERAL NOTES

_____
_____
_____
_____
_____
_____
_____
_____
_____
_____

IN HINDSIGHT...

_____
_____
_____
_____
_____
_____
_____
_____

ALL in ALL, A PRETTY EPIC DAY!

Date: _____

EPIC METER

GENERAL NOTES

_____
_____
_____
_____
_____
_____
_____

IN HINDSIGHT...

_____
_____
_____
_____
_____
_____
_____

ALL in ALL, A PRETTY EPIC DAY!

CURRENT MOOD

JUST YELL it OUT!

HOW DID TODAY MEASURE UP!

TODAY _____

YESTERDA

PRO TIP:

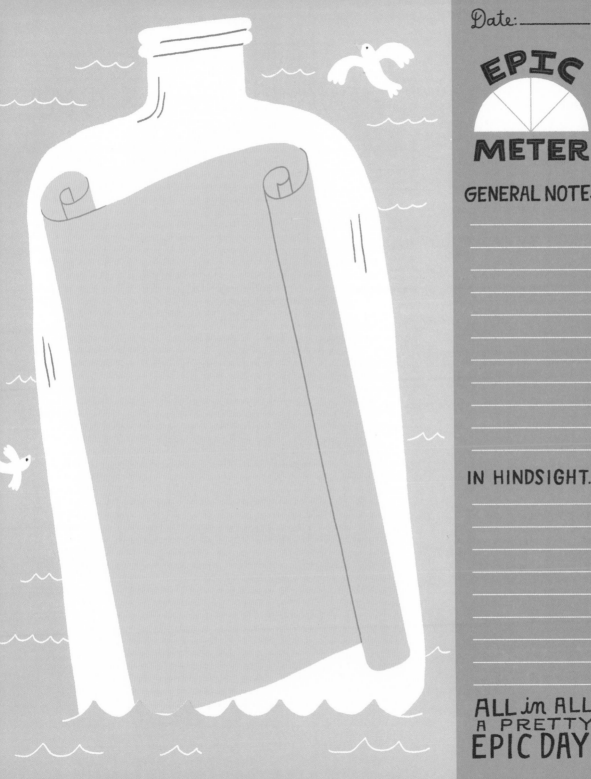

EPIC

METER

GENERAL NOTES
_____
_____
_____
_____
_____
_____
_____
_____
_____
_____
_____

IN HINDSIGHT...
_____
_____
_____
_____
_____
_____
_____
_____

ALL in ALL,
A PRETTY
EPIC DAY!

Date:_____

EPIC METER

GENERAL NOTES

_____
_____
_____
_____
_____
_____
_____
_____
_____
_____

IN HINDSIGHT...

_____
_____
_____
_____
_____
_____

ALL in ALL, A PRETTY EPIC DAY!

EPIC RANT

HOW IS IT POSSIBLE...

_____
_____
_____
_____
_____
_____
_____
_____
_____
_____
_____
_____
_____
_____

Rant Over.

ON SECOND THOUGHT...

_____
_____
_____
_____
_____
_____

CURRENT DAYDREAMS

CURRENT OBSESSION

IT HAS BEEN

DAYS SINCE THE LAST HAPPY ACCIDENT.

IT'S in the BAG!

EPIC METER

GENERAL NOTES

IN HINDSIGHT...

ALL in ALL, A PRETTY EPIC DAY!

Date:_____

EPIC
METER

GENERAL NOTES
_____
_____
_____
_____
_____
_____
_____
_____

IN HINDSIGHT...
_____
_____
_____
_____
_____
_____
_____
_____

ALL *in* ALL,
A PRETTY
EPIC DAY!

CAUTION
AHEAD

OVERHEAR *anything* INTERESTING TODAY?

INTERESTING
★ OBSERVATION ★

GROUNDBREAKING
DISCOVERY

FILL 'ER UP!

ONE STEP at a TIME

EPIC

METER

GENERAL NOTES

IN HINDSIGHT...

ALL in ALL,
A PRETTY
EPIC DAY!

Once Upon Today

The End

TODAY'S HEADLINE

EPIC DAILY

3 WISHES

FRIENDS you're ROOTING for

EPIC METER

GENERAL NOTES

_____
_____
_____
_____
_____
_____
_____
_____
_____

IN HINDSIGHT...

_____
_____
_____
_____
_____
_____
_____
_____
_____

ALL in ALL, A PRETTY EPIC DAY!

Date: _____

EPIC

METER

GENERAL NOTES

_____
_____
_____
_____
_____
_____
_____
_____
_____
_____
_____
_____

IN HINDSIGHT...

_____
_____
_____
_____
_____
_____
_____
_____
_____
_____
_____
_____

ALL in ALL,
A PRETTY
EPIC DAY!

BIG PLANS

WRITE IT DOWN

BEFORE YOU FORGET

LEFTOVER PROBLEMS

EPIC

METER

GENERAL NOTES

_____
_____
_____
_____
_____
_____
_____
_____

IN HINDSIGHT...

_____
_____
_____
_____
_____
_____
_____

ALL in ALL, A PRETTY EPIC DAY!

FILL ANY BIG SHOES TODAY?

OR SMELLY SOCKS?

OR COWBOY BOOTS?

OR BARE FEET?

Date:_____

EPIC

METER

_____
_____
_____
_____
_____
_____
_____
_____
_____

WHAT YOU SAID:

WHAT YOU ACTUALLY wanted TO SAY:

WHAT YOU MEANT TO SAY:

Date:_____

EPIC

METER

_____
_____
_____
_____
_____
_____
_____

HIGH NOTES

HARMONY

LOW NOTES

LADDER to SUCCESS

EPIC METER

GENERAL NOTES

_____
_____
_____
_____
_____
_____
_____
_____
_____
_____

IN HINDSIGHT...

_____
_____
_____
_____
_____
_____
_____
_____
_____

ALL in ALL, A PRETTY EPIC DAY!

Date:_____

EPIC
METER

GENERAL NOTES

_____
_____
_____
_____
_____
_____
_____

IN HINDSIGHT...

_____
_____
_____
_____
_____
_____

ALL *in* ALL,
A PRETTY
EPIC DAY!

SPECIAL REMINDER

🔍 UPON FURTHER INVESTIGATION

SUBJECT:

EXPLANATION

The RESULT

Could this day get any SWEETER?

_____
_____
_____
_____

Sugar NEEDS___more SPOONFULS

Random Act of Kindness

CAUSES WORTH ROOTING FOR

EPIC METER

GENERAL NOTES

_____
_____
_____
_____
_____
_____
_____
_____
_____

IN HINDSIGHT...

_____
_____
_____
_____
_____
_____
_____

ALL in ALL, A PRETTY EPIC DAY!

Date: _____

EPIC
METER

REALLY?! REALLY.

GENERAL NOTES

_____
_____
_____
_____
_____
_____
_____
_____
_____

IN HINDSIGHT...

_____
_____
_____
_____
_____
_____
_____
_____
_____

ALL in ALL, A PRETTY EPIC DAY!

RANT OVER.

SPECIAL KEEPSAKE

NAME THIS CAT

_____

EPIC

METER

GENERAL NOTES

_____
_____
_____
_____
_____
_____
_____
_____
_____
_____

IN HINDSIGHT...

_____
_____
_____
_____
_____
_____
_____

ITEMS THAT ARE STILL LOST

MYSTERIOUSLY MISSING ↗

NEVER LENDING MY STUFF AGAIN...

↖ MISS that ONE...

↖ WHERE COULD IT BE?!

WHY?

HMM...

NOW THAT'S A REASON TO CELEBRATE!

ALL in ALL, A PRETTY EPIC DAY!

Date:_____

EPIC
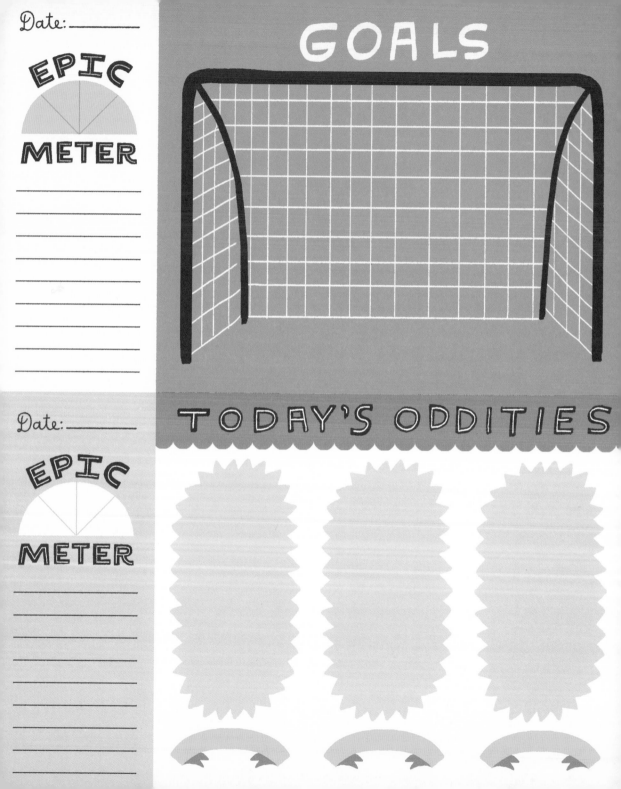
METER

_____
_____
_____
_____
_____
_____
_____
_____
_____

GOALS

Date:_____

EPIC
METER

_____
_____
_____
_____
_____
_____
_____
_____

TODAY'S ODDITIES

Let it SOAK in...

EPIC METER

GENERAL NOTES

_____
_____
_____
_____
_____
_____
_____
_____
_____

IN HINDSIGHT...

_____
_____
_____
_____
_____
_____
_____
_____

ALL in ALL, A PRETTY EPIC DAY!

Date: _____

EPIC METER

GENERAL NOTES

_____
_____
_____
_____
_____
_____
_____
_____
_____

IN HINDSIGHT...

_____
_____
_____
_____
_____
_____
_____
_____

ALL in ALL, A PRETTY EPIC DAY!

TODAY'S ACCOMPLISHMENTS

PROBLEM-REPAIR-SHOP QUEUE

_____
_____
_____
_____
_____
_____
_____

Nothing is unfixable!

TRY to WALK in SOMEONE ELSE'S SHOES

Learn anything on the journey?

_____
_____
_____
_____

HOW did TODAY START?

HOW did TODAY END?

IS EVERYTHING ORGANIZED?

Date: _____

EPIC METER

GENERAL NOTES

_____
_____
_____
_____
_____
_____

IN HINDSIGHT...

_____
_____
_____
_____
_____
_____

ALL in ALL, A PRETTY EPIC DAY!

Date: _____

EPIC METER

GENERAL NOTES

_____
_____
_____
_____
_____
_____
_____
_____
_____

IN HINDSIGHT...

_____
_____
_____
_____
_____
_____
_____
_____

ALL *in* ALL, A PRETTY EPIC DAY!

LIE AWAKE THINKING

Fond Memory

TODAY'S LOG

COUNT YOUR LUCKY STARS

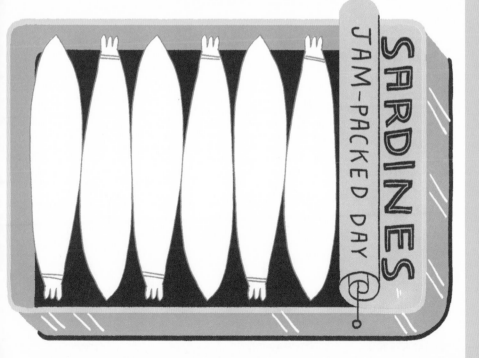

SARDINES — JAM-PACKED DAY

Date: _____

EPIC
METER

GENERAL NOTES

_____
_____
_____
_____
_____
_____
_____
_____

IN HINDSIGHT...

_____
_____
_____
_____
_____
_____
_____

ALL *in* **ALL,**
A PRETTY
EPIC DAY!

PERFORMANCE
RANKING

_____ ROOKIE

_____ NOVICE

_____ EXPERT

_____ VETERAN

_____ GRIZZLED

HATS
OFF
TO YOU

Today's Specials

YOUR

2¢

Date: _____

EPIC METER

GENERAL NOTES

_____
_____
_____
_____
_____
_____
_____
_____
_____
_____
_____
_____

IN HINDSIGHT...

_____
_____
_____
_____
_____
_____
_____
_____
_____

ALL in ALL, A PRETTY EPIC DAY!

Greetings from... SUNNY · RAINY · BORING · EXPENSIVE

_____

WHERE I LEARNED THAT...

_____

EPIC RANT

SING IT!

WORD OF THE DAY

Date: _____

EPIC

METER

GENERAL NOTES

_____
_____
_____
_____
_____
_____
_____
_____
_____

IN HINDSIGHT...

_____
_____
_____
_____
_____
_____
_____
_____

ALL in ALL, A PRETTY EPIC DAY!

BREAKING NEWS

BULLETIN BOARD

LOST

WANTED

FOUND

TODAY, SUMMED UP IN PANTS

STAINED SWEATPANTS

SENSIBLE SLACKS

Sexy leather pants

MESSAGE to the WORLD!

Date:_____

EPIC METER

GENERAL NOTES
_____
_____
_____
_____
_____
_____
_____
_____
_____
_____
_____
_____
_____

IN HINDSIGHT...
_____
_____
_____
_____
_____
_____
_____
_____
_____
_____

ALL in ALL, A PRETTY EPIC DAY!

Date: _____

EPIC

METER

GENERAL NOTES

_____
_____
_____
_____
_____
_____
_____
_____
_____

IN HINDSIGHT...

_____
_____
_____
_____
_____
_____

ALL in ALL, A PRETTY EPIC DAY!

MOOD
FORECAST

WORLD'S BEST

_____

CURRENT
KARAOKE JAM

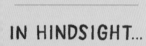

TOMORROW'S PREDICTION

WRITE THE FIRST THING THAT POPS INTO YOUR HEAD.

_____
_____
_____
_____
_____
_____
_____
_____

YUCK!   YUM!

_____
_____
_____
_____
_____
_____
_____
_____

Date: _____

EPIC METER

GENERAL NOTES

_____
_____
_____
_____
_____
_____
_____

IN HINDSIGHT...

_____
_____
_____
_____
_____
_____
_____

ALL *in* ALL,
A PRETTY
EPIC DAY!

VENT HERE

_____ _____
_____ _____
_____ _____
_____ _____

ACCOMPLISHMENTS

MAJOR	MINOR	MEH

HOW CLOSE TO THE TARGET WERE YOU TODAY?

EVERYONE SHOULD...

Date: _____

EPIC METER

GENERAL NOTES

_____
_____
_____
_____
_____
_____
_____
_____
_____
_____
_____
_____
_____
_____

IN HINDSIGHT...

_____
_____
_____
_____
_____
_____
_____
_____
_____
_____
_____
_____

SPICE up THE DAY!

ALL in ALL, A PRETTY EPIC DAY!

Date: _____

EPIC

METER

GENERAL NOTES

_____
_____
_____
_____
_____
_____
_____
_____
_____

IN HINDSIGHT...

_____
_____
_____
_____
_____
_____

ALL in ALL, A PRETTY EPIC DAY!

EPIC RANT

Why do we STILL...

RANT OVER.

ADVICE COLUMN

FEELING STUMPED

IMMENSE PROBLEMS

EPIC METER

GENERAL NOTES

_____
_____
_____
_____
_____
_____
_____
_____

IN HINDSIGHT...

_____
_____
_____
_____
_____
_____
_____
_____

ALL in ALL, A PRETTY EPIC DAY!

Date:_____

EPIC
METER

_____
_____
_____
_____
_____
_____
_____
_____

TODAY'S TAKEAWAY

Date:_____

EPIC
METER

_____
_____
_____
_____
_____
_____
_____
_____

Today's Lesson

TODAY'S TOP 10

10
9
8
7
6
5
4
3
2
1

PRO TIP:

CURRENT
OBSESSION

what are we celebrating?

Date: _____

EPIC METER

GENERAL NOTES

IN HINDSIGHT...

ALL in ALL, A PRETTY EPIC DAY!

Date: _____

EPIC METER

GENERAL NOTES

_____
_____
_____
_____
_____
_____
_____
_____
_____

IN HINDSIGHT...

_____
_____
_____
_____
_____
_____
_____
_____

ALL *in* ALL, A PRETTY EPIC DAY!

RETRACE *your* STEPS

START

1

2

3

4

5

6

7

END

DA BOMB or

TODAY

BOMBED IT?

CURRENT OBSESSION

EPIC

METER

GENERAL NOTES

_____
_____
_____
_____
_____
_____

BIG Announcement

IN HINDSIGHT...

_____
_____
_____
_____
_____
_____
_____
_____

WAS THE GLASS...

- ○ HALF-FULL?
- ○ HALF-EMPTY?
- ○ OVERFLOWING?
- ○ BONE-DRY?

ALL in ALL, A PRETTY EPIC DAY!

Date:_____

EPIC METER

GENERAL NOTES

_____
_____
_____
_____
_____
_____
_____
_____
_____

IN HINDSIGHT...

_____
_____
_____
_____
_____
_____

ALL in ALL, A PRETTY EPIC DAY!

HIGH POINTS of the DAY vs. LOW POINTS

WHAT WILL GO DOWN IN HISTORY TODAY?

THIS SUCKS

_____

(BUT SOON IT WON'T)

CERTIFICATE OF TODAY'S ACCOMPLISHMENTS

EPIC METER

GENERAL NOTES

_____
_____
_____
_____
_____
_____
_____
_____
_____
_____

IN HINDSIGHT...

_____
_____
_____
_____
_____
_____
_____

ALL in ALL, A PRETTY EPIC DAY!

Date: _____

EPIC
METER

_____
_____
_____
_____
_____
_____
_____
_____
_____

GOALS

Date: _____

EPIC
METER

_____
_____
_____
_____
_____
_____
_____
_____
_____

TODAY'S ODDITIES

A NEW PERSPECTIVE

EPIC

METER

GENERAL NOTES

_____
_____
_____
_____
_____
_____
_____
_____
_____

IN HINDSIGHT...

_____
_____
_____
_____
_____
_____
_____
_____

ALL in ALL, A PRETTY EPIC DAY!

Date: _____

GENERAL NOTES

_____
_____
_____
_____
_____
_____
_____
_____
_____
_____

IN HINDSIGHT...

_____
_____
_____
_____
_____
_____
_____

ALL in ALL,
A PRETTY
EPIC DAY!

SOMETHING YOU'VE BEEN MEANING TO GET OFF YOUR BACK:

when life hands you LEMONS, turn them INTO...

EPIC

METER

GENERAL NOTES

_____
_____
_____
_____
_____
_____
_____
_____
_____
_____
_____
_____
_____

IN HINDSIGHT...

_____
_____
_____
_____
_____
_____
_____
_____

TODAY COULD'VE USED AN
°° AUTOMATED °°

01

Where WOULD you HEAD on the OPEN ROAD?

ALL in ALL, A PRETTY EPIC DAY!

Date: _____

EPIC

METER

GENERAL NOTES

_____
_____
_____
_____
_____
_____
_____
_____
_____
_____

IN HINDSIGHT...

_____
_____
_____
_____
_____
_____
_____
_____

ALL in ALL, A PRETTY EPIC DAY!

WISH LIST

SH*T LIST

WHEN THE PLANETS ALIGN

_____
_____
_____
_____
_____

COUNT YOUR LUCKY STARS

SARDINES
JAM-PACKED DAY

Date:_____

EPIC

METER

_____
_____
_____
_____
_____
_____
_____
_____

Date:_____

EPIC

METER

_____
_____
_____
_____
_____
_____
_____

Date: _____

EPIC METER

GENERAL NOTES

_____
_____
_____
_____
_____
_____
_____
_____
_____
_____

IN HINDSIGHT...

_____
_____
_____
_____
_____
_____
_____
_____
_____
_____
_____
_____

ALL in ALL,
A PRETTY
EPIC DAY!

JUST PUTTING THIS
OUT THERE...

TODAY'S
TOP 10

PRO TIP:

10
9
8
7
6
5
4
3
2
1

CURRENT OBSESSION

what are we celebrating?

EPIC METER

GENERAL NOTES

_____
_____
_____
_____
_____
_____
_____
_____
_____
_____

IN HINDSIGHT...

_____
_____
_____
_____
_____
_____
_____
_____
_____

ALL in ALL, A PRETTY EPIC DAY!

EPIC

METER

GENERAL NOTES

_____
_____
_____
_____
_____
_____
_____
_____
_____

IN HINDSIGHT...

_____
_____
_____
_____
_____
_____
_____
_____

ALL in ALL, A PRETTY EPIC DAY!

NOTEWORTHY NEWS

_____
_____

HEY! WHAT'S COOKIN'?

WELL-DONE	HALF-BAKED	OVERDONE

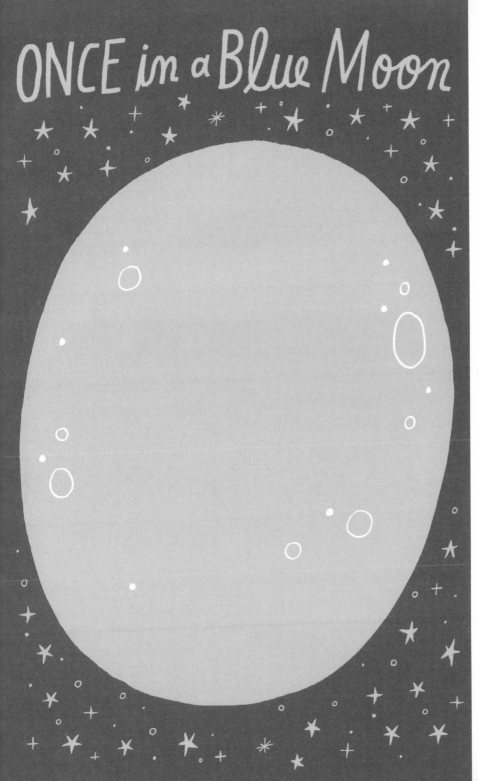

ONCE in a Blue Moon

EPIC
METER

GENERAL NOTES

_____
_____
_____
_____
_____
_____
_____
_____
_____
_____

IN HINDSIGHT...

_____
_____
_____
_____
_____
_____
_____
_____
_____

ALL in ALL,
A PRETTY
EPIC DAY!

Date: _____

EPIC METER

GENERAL NOTES
_____
_____
_____
_____
_____
_____
_____
_____
_____
_____

IN HINDSIGHT...
_____
_____
_____
_____
_____
_____
_____
_____
_____

ALL *in* ALL, A PRETTY EPIC DAY!

FUTURE BUSINESSES

WHAT **HOOPS** DID YOU *HAVE* TO *JUMP* THROUGH TODAY?

BUDDING IDEAS

EXPRESS TICKET

TO:_____

Date: _____

EPIC METER

GENERAL NOTES

_____
_____
_____
_____
_____
_____
_____
_____

IN HINDSIGHT...

_____
_____
_____
_____
_____
_____

ALL in ALL, A PRETTY EPIC DAY!

FRUITS of YOUR LABOR

WALL of FAME

WALL of SHAME

DEEP THOUGHTS

SHIPWRECKS

BURIED TREASURE

EPIC METER

GENERAL NOTES

_____
_____
_____
_____
_____
_____
_____
_____
_____
_____

IN HINDSIGHT...

_____
_____
_____
_____
_____
_____
_____
_____

ALL in ALL, A PRETTY EPIC DAY!

Date: ——————

EPIC METER

GENERAL NOTES

—————————
—————————
—————————
—————————
—————————
—————————
—————————
—————————

IN HINDSIGHT...

—————————
—————————
—————————
—————————
—————————
—————————
—————————
—————————

ALL *in* ALL,
A PRETTY
EPIC DAY!

STEPPING STONES

BUILDING BLOCKS

LOOKING FORWARD TO...

OFFICIAL
COUNTDOWN

(YOUR MESSAGE HERE)

ORGANIZE YOUR THOUGHTS

EPIC METER

GENERAL NOTES

_____
_____
_____
_____
_____
_____
_____
_____
_____
_____

IN HINDSIGHT...

_____
_____
_____
_____
_____
_____
_____

ALL in ALL, A PRETTY EPIC DAY!

Date:————

EPIC
METER

_____
_____
_____
_____
_____
_____
_____
_____

SNAP DECISION
maker

#1 ⬭ #2 ⬭ #3 ⬭

NOPE   YASS!   NAH

Date:————

EPIC
METER

_____
_____
_____
_____
_____
_____
_____

← ↗ ↓

WHERE DID YOU GO?

WHO DID YOU SEE?

↗

WHAT DO YOU KNOW?

↓

↘

↑

→

The TITLE of TODAY'S BOOK

The TITLE of YESTERDAY'S BOOK

EPIC

METER

GENERAL NOTES

_____
_____
_____
_____
_____
_____
_____
_____
_____
_____
_____
_____

WHICH TOOL WILL REPAIR TODAY? (CIRCLE ONE)

IN HINDSIGHT...

_____
_____
_____
_____
_____
_____
_____
_____
_____
_____

THE TUNNEL

THE LIGHT
at the END of IT

ALL in ALL,
A PRETTY
EPIC DAY!

Date:_____

EPIC

METER

GENERAL NOTES

IN HINDSIGHT...

ALL in ALL, A PRETTY EPIC DAY!

Recipe for SUCCESS

Recipe for DISASTER

With a DASH of

and a PINCH of

ADD a TOUCH of

and TOP with

AIR YOUR GRIEVANCES

LIFE REPORT CARD

A-DOING GREAT	B-NOT BAD	C-NEEDS IMPROVEMENT	D-THAT DIDN'T GO WELL	F-UGHH!!

SUBJECT	GRADE

Extra Credit

EPIC
METER

GENERAL NOTES
_____
_____
_____
_____
_____
_____
_____
_____
_____
_____

IN HINDSIGHT...
_____
_____
_____
_____
_____
_____
_____
_____
_____

ALL in ALL,
A PRETTY
EPIC DAY!

Date: _____

EPIC METER

GENERAL NOTES

_____
_____
_____
_____
_____
_____
_____
_____

IN HINDSIGHT...

_____
_____
_____
_____
_____
_____

ALL *in* ALL,
A PRETTY
EPIC DAY!

WINDOWS OF OPPORTUNITY

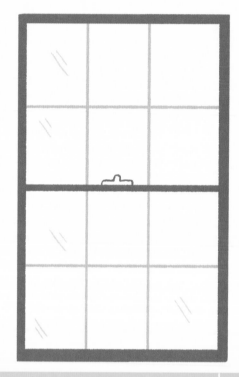

IT WAS THE BEST OF TIMES	IT WAS THE WORST OF TIMES

TODAY'S GOOD EGGS

TODAY'S BAD APPLES

Date:_____

EPIC METER

GENERAL NOTES

_____
_____
_____
_____
_____
_____
_____

IN HINDSIGHT...

_____
_____
_____
_____
_____
_____
_____
_____

ALL *in* ALL,
A PRETTY
EPIC DAY!

Date: _____

EPIC
METER

GENERAL NOTES

_____
_____
_____
_____
_____
_____
_____
_____

IN HINDSIGHT...

_____
_____
_____
_____
_____
_____
_____

ALL in ALL,
A PRETTY
EPIC DAY!

Let it SOAK in...

ABOUT the AUTHOR

Mary Kate McDevitt is a letterer and illustrator based in Philadelphia, Pennsylvania. When she started her freelance career in 2009, she began hand-lettering the motivational phrases that inspired her to start her online shop, promote her work, and get stuff done. Mary Kate still uses the theme of motivation in her work—and believes that if you draw (or write) it enough, it will come true. When not in her studio, Mary Kate is walking around the city collecting ephemera from thrift shops or redecorating her apartment with her boyfriend and cat, or enjoying a cup of coffee. For more, visit marykatemcdevitt.com.

Any day WITH ICE CREAM is pretty EPIC in my BOOK.